THE REVENGE OF THE BABY-SAT

Also by Bill Watterson

Calvin and Hobbes
Something Under the Bed Is Drooling
Yukon Ho!
Weirdos From Another Planet
Lazy Sunday Book
The Authoritative Calvin and Hobbes
Scientific Progress Goes 'Boink'
Attack of the Deranged Mutant Killer Monster Snow Goons
Indispensable Calvin and Hobbes
The Days Are Just Packed
Homicidal Psycho Jungle Cat
The Essential Calvin and Hobbes

Taken from Calvin and Hobbes:

Calvin and Hobbes 1: Thereby Hangs a Tale
Calvin and Hobbes 2: One Day the Wind Will Change
Calvin and Hobbes 3: In the Shadow of the Night

THE REVENGE OF THE BABY-SAT

A Calvin and Hobbes Collection by Bill Watterson

WARNER BOOKS

A *Warner* Book

First published in US by Andrews and McMeel 1991
First published in Great Britain by Sphere Books Ltd 1991
Reprinted 1991, 1992
This edition published by Warner Books in 1992
Reprinted 1993, 1994, 1995

Printed and bound in Great Britain by
BPC Hazell Books Ltd
A member of
The British Printing Company Ltd

ISBN 0 7515 0831 4

Warner Books
A Division of
Little, Brown and Company (UK)
Brettenham House
Lancaster Place
London WC2E 7EN

WHO MADE THIS MESS OUT HERE ?!

IT WASN'T *ME*, MOM! IT WAS...UH.. IT WAS...

IT WAS A HORRIBLE LITTLE VENUSIAN WHO MATERIALIZED IN THE KITCHEN! HE TOOK OUT SOME DIABOLICAL HIGH-FREQUENCY DEVICE, POINTED IT AT VARIOUS OBJECTS, AND...

MOTHERS ARE THE NECESSITY OF INVENTION.

I'M HO-OME!

KAPOW!

WHAT DID YOU DO, STEP ON A LAND MINE?

WHEN'S DAD EVER GOING TO BUILD THAT TIGER PIT I KEEP ASKING HIM ABOUT?

CALVIN, WHERE ARE YOU? GET OUT HERE!

COME ON, CALVIN, I'M GETTING TIRED OF THIS!

I *MEAN* IT, CALVIN! COME OUT AND TAKE YOUR BATH! *NOW!*

SOONER OR LATER SHE'S GOING TO HAVE TO QUESTION WHETHER THIS IS REALLY WORTH THE TROUBLE.

CALVIN and HOBBES
by WATTERSON

IF *I* WAS IN CHARGE, WE'D NEVER SEE GRASS BETWEEN OCTOBER AND MAY.

ON "THREE," READY? ONE... TWO... THREE!

SNOW!

I SAID SNOW! C'MON! SNOW!

SNOW!

OK THEN, *DON'T* SNOW! SEE WHAT *I* CARE! I *LIKE* THIS WEATHER! LET'S HAVE IT FOREVER!

PLEEAASE SNOW! PLEASE?? JUST A FOOT! OK, EIGHT INCHES! THAT'S ALL! C'MON! SIX INCHES, EVEN! HOW ABOUT JUST SIX??

I'M *WAAIIITING...*

RRRRGGHHH

DO YOU WANT ME TO BECOME AN ATHEIST?

SPIFF'S SPACECRAFT IS IMMOBILIZED! THE NAVIGATRON HAS SHORTED OUT!

A ZILLION MILES FROM ANY PLANET, OUR HERO MUST CLIMB OUT AND FIX IT HIMSELF IN ZERO GRAVITY!

UPSIDE DOWN, SPIFF CLINGS TIGHTLY TO HIS SPACE SHIP! ONE SLIP WILL SEND HIM HURLING INTO THE HORRORS OF THE INFINITE BEYOND!

GO...TO... SCHOOL!

NO!

I DON'T UNDERSTAND HOW SANTA RUNS HIS OPERATION. HOW CAN HE AFFORD TO GIVE TOYS AWAY?

HOW DOES HE PAY FOR THE RAW MATERIALS HE USES TO MAKE THE TOYS? HOW DOES HE PAY HIS ELVES?

THERE'S NO INCOME TO COVER HIS COSTS. HOW DOES HE DO IT?

DEFICIT SPENDING, I GUESS.

SURE, BUT SOONER OR LATER IT'S GOING TO CATCH UP TO HIM, AND THEN WHERE WILL I BE?!

DEAR SANTA, HI, IT'S ME, CALVIN. THIS YEAR I'VE BEEN

EXTRA GOOD, SO...

PBTBT!!

MMF MMF EEP!

PERHAPS YOU NEED A DRINK OF WATER.

I THINK I DO.

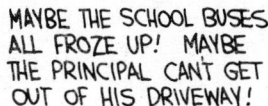

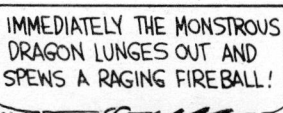

I'm gonna pound you in gym class, shrimp.

GET YOUR KICKS **NOW**, YOU GLANDULAR FREAK, BECAUSE ONCE YOU GROW UP YOU CAN'T GO BEATING PEOPLE UP FOR NO REASON!

Yeah, I guess you're right.

THAT REALLY WASN'T WHAT I MEANT AT ALL.

WHAT GRADE DID YOU GET?

I GOT AN "A."

REALLY? BOY, I'D HATE TO BE YOU. I GOT A "C."

WHY ON EARTH WOULD YOU RATHER GET A "C" THAN AN "A"?!

I FIND MY LIFE IS A LOT EASIER THE LOWER I KEEP EVERYONE'S EXPECTATIONS.

WHY DO I HAVE TO WEAR THESE DORKY CLOTHES AND GET MY HAIR COMBED?!

YOUR DAD'S GOING TO TAKE YOUR PICTURE. HOLD STILL.

I DON'T *WANT* TO GET MY PICTURE TAKEN!

IT WILL JUST TAKE A FEW MINUTES. WE'RE GOING TO PUT THE PICTURE OF YOU IN OUR CHRISTMAS CARDS SO EVERYONE CAN SEE WHAT YOU LOOK LIKE NOW.

WHAT A DUMB IDEA. WHY ARE WE DOING *THAT?*

SO WE WON'T HAVE RELATIVES DROPPING BY TO VISIT.

DEAR...

Calvin and Hobbes

by WATTERSON

AHH... THE PERFECT SLUSHBALL!

HARD ENOUGH TO STING, YET SLOPPY ENOUGH TO DRIBBLE DOWN THE COLLAR AND SOAK THE UNDERGARMENTS.

HERE COMES SUSIE! NOW'S MY CHANCE TO HIT HER WITH A SLUSHBALL!

I SEE YOU! YOU'D BETTER NOT THROW THAT! SANTA CLAUS IS WATCHING YOU RIGHT NOW!

ZINGG

FWISSHHH!

WHAP!

OH YES! YES! IT WAS WORTH IT! WHAT A SHOT! I'M NOT SORRY! OH, IT WAS BEAUTIFUL! I'D DO IT AGAIN IN A MINUTE! HA HA!

SANTA'S GONNA SKIP THIS BLOCK FOR YEARS.

WATTERSON

THERE'S NOTHING PRETTIER THAN NEW FALLEN SNOW ON A CLEAR, FREEZING MOONLIT NIGHT.

... THROUGH A WINDOW, THAT IS.

I CAN'T TAKE A BATH IN THIS! THE WATER'S *BOILING*! I'LL SCALD MYSELF!

WHAT ARE YOU TRYING TO DO, COOK ME ALIVE?? WELL, FORGET IT! I'M NOT GETTING IN!

BY THE TIME YOU QUIT FUSSING, COMPLAINING, YELLING AND SCREAMING, AND ACTUALLY TAKE OFF YOUR CLOTHES AND GET IN, THE WATER WILL BE PERFECT!

BOY, DOES SHE KNOW ME.

EVERY DAY I HAVE TO GET UP AND GO TO SCHOOL.

NOTHING EVER CHANGES. IT'S JUST SCHOOL, SCHOOL, SCHOOL.

BUT NOT TODAY.

TODAY, I GO FOR THE GUSTO.

I THINK YOU SHOULD ASK YOUR MOM IF IT'S OK.

SHOVEL, SHOVEL, SHOVEL!

WHY CAN'T WE GET A SNOW BLOWER?? WE MUST BE THE ONLY FAMILY IN THE WORLD THAT STILL SHOVELS THE DRIVEWAY BY HAND! I'M FREEZING!

IT BUILDS CHARACTER. KEEP AT IT.

PRETTY CONVENIENT HOW EVERY TIME *I* BUILD CHARACTER, *HE* SAVES A COUPLE HUNDRED DOLLARS.

NEXT TIME WE GO DOWN, *I* GET TO STEER THE SLED.

YOU?! YOU STEER LIKE AN OLD LADY!

YEAH, WELL, I'M SICK OF GOING OVER AND THROUGH EVERY OBSTACLE ON THE HILL.

"EVERY OBSTACLE"?!? WE MISSED THE BRIAR PATCH, DIDN'T WE?!

BY GOING DOWN THE GULLY AND INTO THE STREAM, YES.

OH, YOU MAKE EVERYTHING SOUND SO TERRIBLE. YOU SHOULD BE GLAD WE'RE ALIVE.

THIS IS THE FINEST SNOWBALL EVER MADE!

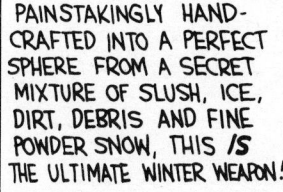

PAINSTAKINGLY HAND-CRAFTED INTO A PERFECT SPHERE FROM A SECRET MIXTURE OF SLUSH, ICE, DIRT, DEBRIS AND FINE POWDER SNOW, THIS *IS* THE ULTIMATE WINTER WEAPON!

YES, THIS MARVEL OF CRYSTALLINE ENGINEERING WI...

WHAP!!

ANOTHER CASUALTY OF THE SEDUCTION OF ART.

WHAT DO YOU THINK IS THE BEST WAY TO GET WHAT YOU WANT? IS IT BETTER TO HOLD FAST AND NEVER BACK DOWN, OR TO COMPROMISE?

I SUPPOSE IT'S BEST TO HOLD FAST WHEN YOU CAN, AND COMPROMISE WHEN YOU NEED TO.

THAT'S A LOT MORE MATURE THAN I THINK I CARE TO BE.

I THINK THE SHORT ATTENTION SPAN OF TELEVISION IS GREAT.

AS FAR AS *I'M* CONCERNED, IF SOMETHING IS SO COMPLICATED THAT YOU CAN'T EXPLAIN IT IN 10 SECONDS, THEN IT'S PROBABLY NOT WORTH KNOWING ANYWAY.

MY TIME IS VALUABLE. I CAN'T GO THINKING ABOUT ONE SUBJECT FOR MINUTES ON END. I'M A BUSY MAN.

...WHO'S BEEN SITTING HERE FOR THREE HOURS.

... AT SIX THOUGHTS A MINUTE.

THERE'S SOMETHING MAGICAL ABOUT HAVING A FIRE.

THE CRACKLES AND SNAPS, THE WARM, FLICKERING LIGHT... EVERYTHING ALWAYS SEEMS SAFE AND COZY IF YOU'RE SITTING IN FRONT OF A FIRE.

AND IF YOU'VE GOT A HOT TIGER TUMMY TO LIE AGAINST.... *WELL!*

21

THE BAY DOORS OPEN AND OUT FALLS CALVIN, THE C·BOMB!

CALVIN IS ABOUT TO UNLEASH THE PURE DESTRUCTIVE FORCE OF A MILLION A·BOMBS!

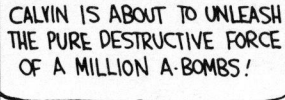

THE WORLD GASPS IN HORROR AS HE STREAKS TOWARD HIS TARGET!

OH NO YOU DON'T.!!

WILL YOU READ THIS TONIGHT?

"AN ODE TO TIGERS"?

HOBBES WROTE IT.

"THE ZEBRA'S STRIPES ARE LACKING HUES, SO THEY DON'T COMPARE TO YOU·KNOW·WHOSE."

"ORANGE, BLACK AND WHITE IS WHAT TO WEAR! IT'S HAUTE COUTURE FOR THOSE WHO DARE! IT'S CAMOUFLAGE, AND STYLISH, TOO! YES, TIGERS LOOK THE BEST, IT'S TRUE!"

THIS GOES ON?

FOR PAGES. PRETTY TEDIOUS, ISN'T IT?

I'M HO-OME!

KAPOW!

WUMPH!

GREAT. THE SNOW CUSHIONED THE BLOW TO MY SPINE, SO NOW I CAN DIE OF PNEUMONIA.

AWW, HAS OO GOT DE SNIFFOOS?

I LIKE THESE COLD, GRAY WINTER DAYS.

DAYS LIKE THESE LET YOU SAVOR A BAD MOOD.

YOU TRY IT AND I'LL WATCH.

SISSY.

LOOK, I PUT A SNOWBALL ON TOP OF THIS SNOWMAN'S HEAD.

NOW I'LL BE THE NEXT WILLIAM TELL, AND I'LL HIT THE SNOWBALL CLEAN OFF!

OUCH.

AHHH! HE FLINCHED!

Calvin and Hobbes

by WATTERSON

OK, LET'S SEE... IF THE WIND IS BLOWING NORTH-NORTHEAST AT 6 MPH, AND I THROW THE SNOWBALL DUE WEST AT 90 MPH WITH A SLIGHT TOP SPIN....

HA! SUSIE DIDN'T EVEN HEAR ME SNEAK UP!

NOW I'LL CREAM HER CRANIUM WITH A BARRAGE OF SNOWBALLS!

WHIZZZ

PIFF

PIFF

THESE DARN CROSS BREEZES! SHE DIDN'T EVEN NOTICE!

YOU'RE THE WORST SHOT IN THE WORLD, CALVIN! IF IT WASN'T FOR GRAVITY, YOU PROBABLY COULDN'T EVEN HIT THE GROUND!

SMACK!

I DID IT! I DID IT! JUST WHEN IT REALLY COUNTED, I DID IT! HA HA HA! RIGHT IN THE KISSER! HA HA!

BAD NEWS, MOM. I PROMISED MY SOUL TO THE DEVIL THIS AFTERNOON.

OH? THAT RECENTLY?

WATTERSON

THE FEARLESS SPACEMAN SPIFF FINDS HIMSELF ON THE PLANET CLOSEST TO STAR X-351!

AN ALIEN APPROACHES... BUT IN THE BLINDING LIGHT, OUR HERO CAN HARDLY MAKE IT OUT! IS IT FRIENDLY OR HOSTILE?

WHAT ARE YOU DOING IN BED STILL?! GET READY FOR SCHOOL!

DEFINITELY HOSTILE.

THE SCHOOL BUS WILL BE HERE ANY MINUTE! GO! SCOOT!

SPACEMAN SPIFF, CAPTURED BY VICIOUS ZOGWARGS, IS ABOUT TO BE TRANSPORTED TO THE LABOR CAMP! OUR HERO HATCHES A BOLD PLAN!

AT THE LAST SECOND, SPIFF MAKES HIS BREAK! TAKING ADVANTAGE OF THE PLANET'S WEAKER GRAVITY, OUR HERO IS AWAY LIKE A SHOT.

THERE'S THE BUS... BUT WHY DON'T I SEE CALVIN?

SPIFF ESCAPES!

DID CALVIN GET ON THE BUS?

I DIDN'T SEE. ...WHY?

SOMEONE JUST DARTED BEHIND THAT TREE. SEE, THERE HE GOES AGAIN! ISN'T THAT CALVIN?

THE ZOGWARGS HAVE SPOTTED HIM! OUR HERO INFLATES THE EMERGENCY JET PACK HE KEEPS IN HIS POCKET, AND PREPARES FOR TAKEOFF!

YES, CAN I HAVE THE TOOL DEPARTMENT, PLEASE? THANK YOU.

HELLO? HOW MUCH ARE YOUR POWER CIRCULAR SAWS? I SEE. AND YOUR ELECTRIC DRILLS? UH-HUH. HOW BIG OF A BIT WILL THAT HOLD? REALLY? GREAT.

SO THE ASSIGNMENT IS PAGES TWO THROUGH FOUR? OK, THANKS SUSIE.

..SORRY ABOUT THAT. DO YOU CARRY ACETYLENE TORCHES? OK, RING IT ALL UP. THIS WILL BE ON MASTERCARD.

LOOK AT ALL THIS HOMEWORK I'M SUPPOSED TO DO!

I DON'T WANT TO DO THIS GARBAGE! I WANT TO GO PLAY OUTSIDE!

CHILDHOOD IS SHORT AND MATURITY IS FOREVER.

PEOPLE ARE ROTTEN.

WHEN I GROW UP, I'M GOING TO LIVE A MILLION MILES AWAY FROM EVERYONE!

HOW WILL YOU SURVIVE? WHAT WILL YOU EAT?

..WELL, MOM COULD COME BY TWICE A DAY TO COOK, I SUPPOSE.

THAT WOULD BE QUITE A COMMUTE.

GET A LOAD OF *THIS* DUMB ASSIGNMENT! I'M SUPPOSED TO WRITE ABOUT AN ADVENTURE I'VE HAD!

I HAVEN'T HAD ANY ADVENTURES! MY LIFE HAS BEEN ONE BIG BORE FROM THE BEGINNING!

HAVE I EVER BEEN ABDUCTED BY PIRATES? HAVE I EVER FACED DOWN A CHARGING RHINO? HAVE I EVER BEEN IN A SHOOT-OUT, OR ON A BOMBING RAID? **NO!** I NEVER GET TO HAVE ADVENTURES!

WHAT ABOUT THE TIME YOU BACKED THE CAR THROUGH THE GARAGE DOOR?

YOU CALL THAT AN ADVENTURE? I DIDN'T EVEN GET ON THE HIGHWAY.

WHEN DO YOU THINK WE'LL GET A THUNDER AND LIGHTNING STORM?

I DON'T KNOW. PROBABLY NOT UNTIL SPRING.

I THINK HE'S GOING TO MELT BEFORE WE CAN BRING HIM TO LIFE.

HEY, SUSIE, STAND ON THIS "X."

WHY?

NO REASON. JUST DO IT. I DARE YOU.

NO.

PLEASE? C'MON!

GET LOST.

THIS MAY NOT WORK OUT AS WELL AS I THOUGHT.

WOW, YOU'VE MADE A LOT OF SNOWMEN TODAY!

YEP. THEY'RE EFFIGIES. EACH ONE REPRESENTS SOMEONE I HATE.

WHEN THE SUN COMES OUT, I'LL WATCH THEIR FEATURES SLOWLY MELT DOWN THEIR DRIPPING BODIES UNTIL THEY'RE NOTHING BUT NOSES AND EYES FLOATING IN POOLS OF WATER.

I WASN'T AWARE YOU EVEN KNEW THIS MANY PEOPLE.

THE ONES I *REALLY* HATE ARE SMALL, SO THEY'LL GO FASTER.

I'M WRITING A BOOK ABOUT MY LIFE.

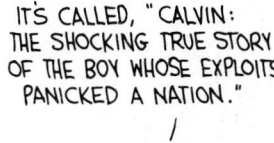

IT'S CALLED, "CALVIN: THE SHOCKING TRUE STORY OF THE BOY WHOSE EXPLOITS PANICKED A NATION."

INTERESTING TITLE.

THANKS.

SPECIFICALLY WHAT EXPLOITS ARE YOU REFERRING TO?

THAT'S THE PROBLEM. CAN YOU HELP ME THINK OF SOME I COULD DO?

HI, SUSIE.

GO AWAY, CALVIN! SIT SOMEWHERE ELSE! I DON'T WANT TO KNOW WHAT REVOLTING THING YOU HAVE FOR LUNCH TODAY.

RELAX, SUSIE. I'M NOT GOING TO TELL YOU WHAT I HAVE.

YOU'D BETTER NOT. I MEAN IT.

ALL I'LL SAY IS THAT I SURE FEEL SORRY FOR MY TAPEWORM.

MISS WORMWOOD!

HEY! DID I *SAY* WHAT MY LUNCH IS?! *DID* I ?!?

CALVIN and HOBBES

by WATTERSON

WHAT'S THIS?

A CRASH TEST DUMMY. NOW I CAN SEE IF THE HILL IS SAFE TO GO DOWN.

OFF YOU GO!

OOH, I THINK I'M GOING TO BE SICK.

WELL I WOULDN'T HAVE STEERED LIKE *THAT!* HE DESERVED IT!

OH, NO! THE AIR PRESSURE IN THIS ROOM IS TOO HIGH!

CALVIN'S ORGANS ARE IN DANGER OF COLLAPSING! HE...HE'S ABOUT TO IMPLODE!

WE'VE GOT TO GET OUT OF HERE! THERE'S TOO MUCH ATMOSPHERE!

SIT STILL AND BEHAVE. WE CAN'T EAT AT FAST FOOD PLACES ALL THE TIME.

THESE TELEVISION PROGRAMS SURE ARE ROTTEN.

THERE ISN'T AN OUNCE OF IMAGINATION IN THE WHOLE BUNCH. WHAT BILGE.

WHO DO THEY THINK IS STUPID ENOUGH TO SIT AND WATCH THIS TRASH?

YOU.

IF THERE WAS ANYTHING *BETTER* ON, I'D WATCH *THAT.*

YOU'RE TAKING A SHOWER *NOW?* THAT MEANS YOU'RE GOING OUT TONIGHT, RIGHT?

AND YOU HAVEN'T TOLD *ME* TO GET CLEANED UP, SO THAT MEANS I'M STAYING HOME, RIGHT?

AND IF I'M STAYING HOME, THAT MEANS YOU'VE GOTTEN ME A BABY SITTER, RIGHT? AND THAT MEANS YOU'VE PROBABLY HIRED *ROSALYN*, RIGHT?!?

BRILLIANT, HOLMES.

AAAHH HAHH!

QUICK, HOBBES! WE'VE GOT TO HIDE! MOM AND DAD GOT *ROSALYN* FOR OUR BABY SITTER AGAIN! AND YOU KNOW WHAT *THAT* MEANS!

IT USUALLY MEANS WE'RE IN BED BY 6:30.

RIGHT! NO TV, NO HORSING AROUND, *NOTHING!* SHE JUST WALKS IN AND SENDS US STRAIGHT TO BED!

AND THEN SHE DOESN'T EVEN KISS US GOOD NIGHT.

EWW, GROSS! YOU *WANT* HER TO?!?

WHERE ARE YOU GOING TONIGHT? WHY CAN'T HOBBES AND I COME? WHY DO WE HAVE TO HAVE A BABY SITTER?

WE'RE GOING TO DINNER AND A MOVIE JUST TO HAVE SOME TIME TO OURSELVES, OK?

BUT WE COULD COME! HOBBES PROMISES NOT TO KILL ANYONE! WE'D BE GOOD! REALLY! WHY WON'T YOU LET US COME? WHY DON'T YOU WANT US AROUND?

IS THE MOVIE DIRTY? WHAT'S THE PROBLEM?!

GOSH, A DINNER WITH REAL PAUSES IN THE CONVERSATION! CAN YOU IMAGINE?

CALVIN, YOU'VE GOT TWO SECONDS TO UNLOCK THIS DOOR AND GIVE ME BACK MY SCIENCE NOTES!

YOU KNOW, ROSALYN, I'D SUGGEST YOU ADOPT A MORE HUMBLE ATTITUDE. YOU WOULDN'T WANT ANYTHING TO *HAPPEN* TO THESE NOTES, WOULD YOU?

YOU SCUMMY LITTLE TROLL! WHEN YOUR PARENTS GET HOME, I'LL...

FLUSH AUGH!

THERE'S *ONE* PAGE!

YOU'D BETTER NOT HAVE REALLY FLUSHED ANY OF MY NOTES! I'VE GOT A BIG TEST TOMORROW!

WELL THEN, WITH THAT AT STAKE, OUR DEMANDS SHOULD SEEM VERY REASONABLE!

DEMANDS?! YOU DON'T GET ANY DEMANDS! UNLOCK THIS DOOR!

BOY, YOU'D THINK A HIGH SCHOOL SENIOR WOULD CATCH ON QUICKER. WE SHOULD WRITE THE SCHOOL BOARD.

TORPEDO TUBE READY, CAP'N!

I SURE HOPE YOU MEMORIZED THIS PAGE ALREADY, BECAUSE YOU'RE NEVER GOING TO SEE IT AGAIN!

NO! DON'T FLUSH IT! TELL ME WHAT YOUR STUPID DEMANDS ARE.

THAT'S MORE LIKE IT! OK, FIRST WE WANT TO STAY UP UNTIL MY PARENTS DRIVE IN. SECOND, WE WANT YOU TO GO PICK UP A PIZZA AND RENT US A VIDEO PLAYER...

YOU'RE OUT OF YOUR MIND!

THIRD ... ARE YOU WRITING THESE DOWN?

CALVIN and HOBBES by WATTERSON

WHAT'S THIS?

A CALVIN DECOY. PRETTY GOOD, HUH?

NOW I CAN FIND OUT WHO MY ENEMIES ARE! I'LL HIDE BEHIND THAT TREE OVER THERE AND WATCH TO SEE WHO THROWS SNOWBALLS AT THE DECOY, THINKING IT'S ME!

YOUR ENEMIES MUST NOT BE VERY BRIGHT.

THAT'S WHY THEY'RE OUT TO GET ME. THEY CAN'T STAND MY GENIUS.

HEY, CALVIN! I SEE A WAY YOUR PLAN MIGHT FAIL.

PIPE DOWN, WILL YA? HOW CAN I HIDE WHEN YOU'RE YELLING TO ME FROM ACROSS...

SMACK!

SEE THERE? MY PLAN TO DISCOVER MY ENEMIES WAS A COMPLETE SUCCESS.

TOO BAD YOU TOOK OFF YOUR COAT AND HAT. YOU MUST BE SOAKED.

Panel 1: HERE WE ARE, POISED ON THE PRECIPICE OF "SUICIDE SLOPE." BELOW US LIE THE SKELETAL REMAINS OF HUNDREDS OF LITTLE SLED RIDERS.

Panel 2: SEARCHING FOR THAT ULTIMATE ADRENALINE RUSH, WE PREPARE TO HURL OURSELVES OVER THE BRINK! WHAT FATE AWAITS US?

Panel 3: READY? / NO.

Panel 4: LIFE AND DEATH HANG IN THE BALANCE! A FRACTION OF A SECOND AND ONE WRONG TURN ARE ALL THAT SEPARATE THEM! / THIS ISN'T HELPING.

Panel 5: DAD SAYS THE ANTICIPATION OF HAVING SOMETHING IS OFTEN MORE FUN THAN ACTUALLY HAVING IT.

Panel 6: I THINK HE'S CRAZY. I HATE WAITING FOR THINGS. I LIKE TO HAVE EVERYTHING IMMEDIATELY.

Panel 7: I CAN'T THINK OF *ANY*THING I'D RATHER ANTICIPATE THAN HAVE RIGHT AWAY. CAN YOU?

Panel 8: DEATH COMES TO MIND. / I DON'T KNOW WHY I BOTHER TRYING TO HAVE A LITTLE DISCUSSION WITH YOU WHEN YOU'RE ALWAYS SO MORBID.

Panel 9: I WISH SNOW WAS DRY, SO THAT YOU DIDN'T GET ALL COLD AND WET WHEN YOU PLAYED IN IT.

Panel 10: ...THEN AGAIN, IF SNOW WAS DRY, YOU COULDN'T PACK IT INTO SNOWBALLS. THAT WOULDN'T BE GOOD.

Panel 11: I WISH IT SNOWED IN SUMMER. WOULDN'T THAT BE FUN? ...WELL NO, ACTUALLY THAT WOULD MAKE IT HARD TO RUN WHEN YOU PLAY BASEBALL.

Panel 12: HECK, IT'S OK JUST THE WAY IT IS. / WE'RE GLAD YOU APPROVE.

CALVIN and HOBBES by WATTERSON

THE PTERANODON SPREADS HIS GIANT WINGS, AND..

1½ BOXES TO GO, AND I'LL HAVE ENOUGH "PROOF OF PURCHASE SEALS" TO ORDER THE PROPELLER BEANIE THEY OFFER.

1⅓ BOXES TO GO.

MAN, I'M *EARNING* THIS.

HOBBES, I DID IT! I ATE ENOUGH BOXES OF CEREAL TO GET ALL THE PROOF OF PURCHASE SEALS I NEED!

NOW I CAN ORDER MY BEANIE! OH, BOY! I CAN'T WAIT TO GET IT! I'LL BE SO COOL!

NOT FOR OVER A MONTH. IT SAYS TO ALLOW SIX WEEKS FOR DELIVERY.

SIX WEEKS ?!?

I'LL BE *OLD* THEN!

AND I'M SURE YOUR BEANIE WILL BE THE TALK OF THE REST HOME.

SCHOOL

MOM! MOM! DID MY BEANIE COME IN THE MAIL?

ARE YOU KIDDING? I JUST MAILED YOUR ORDER THIS MORNING.

I'M NEVER GOING TO MAKE IT SIX WEEKS.

I CAN'T BELIEVE THIS. EVERY DAY I GET ALL MY HOPES UP, THINKING MY BEANIE WILL COME... AND THEN IT DOESN'T.

AND FOR EACH DAY THAT GOES BY, I FIGURE THE ODDS ARE BETTER THAT IT WILL COME THE *NEXT* DAY, SO MY HOPES GET HIGHER AND HIGHER BEFORE THEY FALL. IT'S AWFUL.

BUT I'VE BEEN DISAPPOINTED SO OFTEN NOW, I'M FINALLY GETTING NUMB TO IT.

MAYBE THE MAILMAN MADE A SECOND TRIP TODAY AND DELIVERED IT IN THE LAST FIVE MINUTES.

WOW! I NEVER THOUGHT OF THAT! C'MON!

HE'S NOT NUMB.

THE LONGER YOU WAIT FOR THE MAIL, THE LESS THERE IS IN IT.

I'M HOME. I DIDN'T GET MY PROPELLER BEANIE TODAY, DID I?

AS A MATTER OF FACT, YOU DID!

IT'S HERE!

HA HA! IT TOOK WEEKS AND WEEKS OF WAITING, BUT AT LONG LAST IT'S HERE! NOW I FINALLY, *FINALLY* GET TO PUT IT ON!

"SOME ASSEMBLY REQUIRED. BATTERIES NOT INCLUDED."

CAN YOU BELIEVE THIS? I'VE GOT TO ASSEMBLE MY BEANIE PROPELLER AND MOTOR MYSELF!

WHAT DO THEY THINK I AM, AN ENGINEER? LOOK, I'VE GOT TO INSERT THESE WIRES AND THIS PLASTIC SWITCH! I CAN'T DO THIS!

HERE, LET ME TRY.

NO! GET AWAY! *I'LL* DO IT! YOU'D PROBABLY GOOF IT ALL UP, OR...

SNAP

OH NO!

SEE? INSULT A TIGER AND YOU GET BAD LUCK! EVERY TIME!

MY MOTOR BROKE! THE PIECE SNAPPED! NOW MY BEANIE PROPELLER WON'T WORK!!

AAGHHGHHH! I WAITED *WEEKS* FOR THIS AND NOW IT'S *BROKEN*, AND I DIDN'T EVEN GET TO *WEAR* IT! STUPID ROTTEN PIECE OF LOUSY *JUNK!!*

IT'S ALL *YOUR* FAULT! RRGHH GHHGH!

MY FAULT?! I WAS JUST SITTING HERE! *YOU* BROKE IT!

YOU *WILLED* ME TO BREAK IT! YOU DID SOME SUBLIMINAL THING! DON'T DENY IT! I KNOW YOU DID! YOU *MUST* HAVE!

OK, *NOW* I'M WILLING YOU TO GO JUMP IN THE SEPTIC TANK.

WHAT ARE YOU MAD AT *ME* FOR?!

GET AWAY FROM ME! I DON'T EVEN WANT TO TALK TO YOU!

YOU BROKE YOUR BEANIE MOTOR, NOT *ME*! I DIDN'T DO ANYTHING!

YOU DISTRACTED ME!

I DID NOT! I WAS JUST *SITTING* HERE! YOU BROKE IT ALL BY YOURSELF!

SNIFF *SNIFFLE* ...ALL RIGHT.. I KNOW..

BUT CONSIDERING MY LIFE'S IN SHAMBLES RIGHT NOW, COULDN'T YOU AT LEAST TAKE THE BLAME?

Panel 1: DAD, CAN YOU FIX MY BEANIE? I BROKE THE PROPELLER MOTOR TRYING TO PUT IT TOGETHER.

WELL, LET'S SEE.

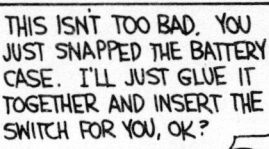

Panel 2: THIS ISN'T TOO BAD. YOU JUST SNAPPED THE BATTERY CASE. I'LL JUST GLUE IT TOGETHER AND INSERT THE SWITCH FOR YOU, OK?

Panel 3: THERE! GOOD AS NEW! NOW JUST LET THIS SIT AWHILE SO THE GLUE CAN SET.

Panel 4: YOU DID IT! YOU FIXED IT! I CAN'T BELIEVE IT! *HEY, MOM!* DAD FIXED SOMETHING!

HE *DID??* YOUR *DAD??*

ALL RIGHT! THAT'S ENOUGH!

Panel 5: LOOK, HOBBES! DAD FIXED MY BEANIE!

Panel 6: WELL? HOW'S IT LOOK?

ADJECTIVES FAIL ME.

Panel 7: I'M TURNING IT ON. READY? HERE GOES.

Panel 8: I DON'T SEEM TO BE LIFTING OFF. THIS IS VERY PECULIAR.

THAT'S THE WORD I WAS LOOKING FOR.

THBBTPTHBB

Panel 9: I'M NOT FLYING! THIS BEANIE DOESN'T MAKE ME FLY!

Panel 10: WHAT'S THE POINT OF A PROPELLER BEANIE IF YOU CAN'T EVEN FLY WHEN YOU WEAR IT?!

NOT "STYLE," CERTAINLY.

Panel 11: WHAT A RIP-OFF! I ATE ALL THAT CEREAL, WAITED WEEKS AND WEEKS TO GET THE BEANIE, ASSEMBLED IT MYSELF, AND THE DUMB THING DOESN'T EVEN FLY!

Panel 12: AT LEAST IT'S NOT A *TOTAL* LOSS. IT CAME IN THIS GREAT CARDBOARD BOX.

OH, BOY! *NOW* WE'LL HAVE SOME FUN!

CALVIN and HOBBES by WATTERSON

I CAN NEVER ENJOY SUNDAYS, BECAUSE IN THE BACK OF MY MIND I ALWAYS KNOW I'VE GOT TO GO TO SCHOOL THE NEXT DAY.

IT'S LIKE TRYING TO ENJOY YOUR LAST MEAL BEFORE THE EXECUTION.

A PENNY FOR YOUR THOUGHTS

SORRY. *MY* THOUGHTS ARE A BUCK APIECE.

A DOLLAR?! THAT'S OUTRAGEOUS! YOUR THOUGHTS AREN'T WORTH THAT!

THIS ONE IS! AT A DOLLAR, IT'S THE BARGAIN OF A LIFETIME.

I WOULDN'T PAY A NICKEL FOR ANY THOUGHT YOU'VE EVER HAD IN YOUR WHOLE FLEA-RIDDEN EXISTENCE!

THAT LITTLE REMARK JUST MADE THE PRICE *TEN* DOLLARS!

TEN?? YOU CAN'T EXTORT ME! *KEEP* YOUR STUPID THOUGHT!

IF YOU KNEW WHAT IT WAS, YOU'D *BEG* TO PAY TEN BUCKS FOR IT.

C'MON, JUST TELL ME WHAT IT IS, WILL YOU?

NOTHING DOING, PAL.

OK, OK! I'LL GIVE YOU 25 CENTS. THAT'S ALL I HAVE.

LET'S SEE IT.

HERE! 25 CENTS! NOW WHAT'S THIS BIG, EXPENSIVE THOUGHT OF YOURS?!

"A FOOL AND HIS MONEY ARE SOON PAR..."

WATTERSON

C'MON, CALVIN! THIS IS THE THIRD TIME I'VE CALLED YOU. GET UP.

I DON'T WANT TO GET UP. I DON'T WANT TO GO TO SCHOOL.

WELL, YOU *HAVE* TO, WHETHER YOU WANT TO OR NOT, SO LET'S MOVE.

FOR YOUR INFORMATION, I DON'T *HAVE* TO DO ANYTHING I DON'T *WANT* TO DO.

IS THAT SO?

SHE SURE CAN MAKE SOMEONE WANT TO DO SOMETHING.

I DON'T WANT TO CATCH THE BUS. I DON'T WANT TO GO TO SCHOOL. I DON'T WANT TO BE HERE AT ALL.

I'M SICK OF EVERYONE TELLING ME WHAT TO DO ALL THE TIME! I HATE MY LIFE! I HATE EVERYTHING! I WISH I WAS *DEAD!*

... WELL, NO, I DON'T. NOT REALLY.

I WISH EVERYONE *ELSE* WAS DEAD.

HI, CALVIN.

HMPH.

OH, *YOU'RE* REAL PLEASANT THIS MORNING. WHAT'S THE MATTER WITH YOU?

GO STEP IN FRONT OF A CEMENT MIXER, OK?

WHAT A PILL YOU ARE! WHAT A JERK! WELL, WHO NEEDS *YOU?!* YOU CAN JUST STAND THERE AND BE GRUMPY ALL BY YOURSELF!

HMPH.

NOTHING HELPS A BAD MOOD LIKE SPREADING IT AROUND.

HOW DID YOU MOUNT YOUR INSECTS, SUSIE?

IN THIS BOX WITH PINS.

HMM... I DON'T HAVE A BOX OR PINS. I GUESS I'LL JUST STICK MY BUGS ON NOTEBOOK PAPER.

OOPS. TAPE DOESN'T WORK TOO WELL. GROSS. I HOPE I CAN GET HIM BACK TOGETHER.

CAN I BORROW YOUR PASTE?

THE WAY YOU'RE GOING, MAYBE YOU'D PREFER A STAPLER.

PSST...SUSIE! HELP ME THINK UP SCIENTIFIC NAMES OF MY BUGS WHILE THE TEACHER'S NOT LOOKING.

SHHH! WE'RE NOT SUPPOSED TO TALK IN CLASS. DO IT YOURSELF.

HAVING A PLEASANT CONVERSATION, MISS DERKINS?

EEEP!

PERHAPS YOU'D LIKE TO SIT UP FRONT, SO YOU WON'T DISTRACT CALVIN ANYMORE.

OH, I *TRIED* TO GET HER TO BE QUIET, BUT YOU KNOW HOW GIRLS ARE.

OOOOH, THAT ROTTEN CALVIN! I HATE HIM! I HATE HIM!

HE'S* THE ONE WHO DIDN'T DO THE ASSIGNMENT! *HE'S* THE ONE WHO WAS TALKING IN CLASS! *HE'S* THE ONE WHO SHOULD BE SITTING HERE AT THE FRONT OF THE ROOM, NOT *ME!

***I* WASN'T DOING ANYTHING WRONG, BUT *I'M* THE ONE WHO GOT IN TROUBLE! I SURE HOPE CALVIN FEELS TERRIBLE ABOUT THIS!**

Hey Susie,
How's the View way up there? Ha! Ha!
Calvin
P.S. try to steal a chalkboard eraser for me.

HERE COMES SUSIE, BACK FROM THE PRINCIPAL'S OFFICE. BOY, DOES SHE LOOK PALE. I WONDER WHAT HAPPENED. SHE'S TALKING TO THE TEACHER NOW.

PSST! SUSIE, WHAT DID THEY DO TO YOU? DID YOU GET EXPELLED? YOU DIDN'T SNITCH ON *ME*, DID YOU?

YOU *DID* SNITCH! YOU'RE A *STOOLIE!* A CANARY!

YOU'RE GOING UP THE RIVER, CALVIN.

CALVIN, WILL YOU COME HERE, PLEASE?

SO *FIRST* I GOT IN TROUBLE FOR NOT PAYING ATTENTION IN CLASS AND FOR TURNING IN A LAST-MINUTE INSECT COLLECTION, WHICH I GOT A "D-MINUS-MINUS" ON.

THEN I GOT IN TROUBLE FOR GETTING *SUSIE* IN TROUBLE WHEN I WANTED HER TO HELP ME FUDGE THE PROJECT.

THEN I GOT IN TROUBLE WHEN I TOLD MOM, AND *THEN* I GOT IN TROUBLE *AGAIN* WHEN *SHE* TOLD *DAD!* I'VE BEEN IN HOT WATER EVER SINCE I GOT UP!

WOW. I'LL BET ALL THIS MAKES YOU GET YOUR BOOK REPORT FINISHED RIGHT ON TIME.

MY WHAT?

ONE OF NATURE'S MOST PECULIAR-LOOKING CREATURES, THE GIRAFFE IS UNIQUELY SUITED TO ITS ENVIRONMENT.

HIS TREMENDOUS HEIGHT ENABLES HIM TO MUNCH ON THE SUCCULENT MORSELS MOST DIFFICULT TO REACH.

CALVIN and HOBBES

by WATTERSON

SIGHHHHHH...

SIGHHHHHH...

GOTCHA!!

HEY! JUST WHAT DO YOU THINK YOU'RE DOING BACK DOWN HERE?!

YOU DIDN'T READ ME MY RIGHTS.

DAD! DAD! OUTER SPACE ALIENS JUST LANDED IN THE BACK YARD!

OH, REALLY. WHAT DO THEY LOOK LIKE?

SORT OF LIKE BIG BAKED POTATOES WITH LASER GUNS. I THINK WE SHOULD DO WHAT THEY SAY.

DID THEY SAY WHAT THEY WANT?

YEAH, THEY WANT 10 DOLLARS.

I'LL BET THEY DO.

SINCE YOU'RE SO BUSY, YOU CAN JUST GIVE THE MONEY TO ME, AND I'LL TAKE IT OVER TO THEM.

CALViN and HOBBES

by WATTERSON

GET UP, CALVIN! I'M NOT GOING TO CALL YOU AGAIN!

I BET.
....

YOU'RE GOING TO MISS THE BUS! NOW GET OUT OF BED!

YOU DON'T KNOW THE ANSWER? THEN SIT DOWN.

12
- 7

Hey, Twinky, want to see if there's an afterlife?

NO, YOU CAN'T GO PLAY UNTIL YOU FINISH YOUR HOMEWORK.

JUST EAT YOUR FOOD. YOU DON'T NEED TO PLAY WITH IT.

STOP STALLING AND GET IN THE BATHTUB.

NO, YOU CAN'T STAY UP A LITTLE LONGER. GO TO BED.

HAVE A GOOD NIGHT'S SLEEP. TOMORROW'S ANOTHER BIG DAY!

... SIGHHHHHH ...

CALVIN and HOBBES
by WATTERSON

THREE... TWO... ONE...

LIGHT SPEED!

BLASTING ACROSS THE GALAXY IN HYPER LIGHT DRIVE, IT'S *SPACEMAN SPIFF*, INTERPLANETARY EXPLORER EXTRAORDIN...

SINCE CALVIN SEEMS TO BE ENJOYING THE LESSON, LET'S HAVE HIM DEMONSTRATE THE NEXT PROBLEM.

ZOUNDS! A ZOK DEATH SLOOP APPEARS OUT OF NOWHERE AND FRIES SPIFF'S STABILIZERS!

OUR HERO HURLS OUT OF CONTROL TOWARD HIS IMMINENT DOOM!

THE SITUATION IS DESPERATE! THIS COULD BE THE END! WHAT CAN OUR HERO DO??

HIS MIND RACING FURIOUSLY, SPIFF SPRINGS INTO ACTION! HE DOWNSHIFTS HIS SPACECRAFT AND...

... STALLS.

RINGG!

OH, DARN, OUT OF TIME.

ONCE AGAIN SPACEMAN SPIFF BEATS ALL ODDS TO SAVE THE DAY!

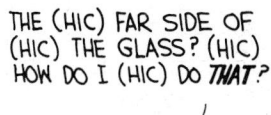

OH MY GOSH!! SOMEBODY BROKE INTO OUR HOUSE!!

I'LL CALL THE POLICE!

WHERE'S HOBBES?

I CAN'T BELIEVE THIS IS HAPPENING! LOOK AT THIS ROOM!

HOBBES! OH, I KNEW WE SHOULDN'T HAVE LEFT HIM HERE!

MOM, I CAN'T FIND HOBBES! HELP ME FIND HIM! WHAT IF... WHAT IF THEY...

IT'S OK, CALVIN. CALM DOWN. I'M SURE HOBBES IS HERE SOME- WHERE.

I DON'T THINK ANYONE WOULD STEAL A STUFFED TIGER. C'MON, LET'S GO LOOK.

BUT HOBBES IS SO TRUSTING..

SNIFF

THE POLICE SAY THEY'LL SEND SOMEONE OVER. HAVE YOU FIGURED OUT WHAT ALL IS MISSING?

NO, WE'RE LOOKING FOR HOBBES. CALVIN'S ALMOST HYSTERICAL.

I FEEL A LITTLE HYSTER- ICAL MYSELF.

OOH...I HOPE THE POLICE GET HERE QUICK. I'M SCARED.

THIS IS ONE OF THOSE THINGS YOU ALWAYS FIGURE WILL HAPPEN TO SOMEONE ELSE.

...UNFORTUNATELY, WE'RE ALL "SOMEONE ELSE" TO SOMEONE ELSE.

HOBBES? HOBBES? WHERE ARE YOU??

I TOLD MOM AND DAD WE LEFT HOBBES BEHIND.... I TRIED TO GET THEM TO TURN AROUND AND COME BACK.... AND NOW LOOK, HOBBES WAS ALL ALONE WHEN OUR HOUSE WAS BROKEN INTO!

MOM SAYS HOBBES WOULDN'T HAVE BEEN STOLEN BECAUSE HE'S NOT VALUABLE.

...(SNIFF) WELL, I THINK HE'S VALUABLE.

HOBBES? ARE YOU DOWN HERE? YOU'VE GOT TO BE *SOME*WHERE!

HERE HE IS, CALVIN! I FOUND HOBBES!

YOU *FOUND* HIM! IS HE OK?? HE'S NOT HURT, IS HE?

HE'S FINE. HE WAS UNDER THE BED COVERS.

HOBBES, I'M SO GLAD TO SEE YOU!! YOU'RE SAFE AND SOUND! (SNIFF) AND NOW I AM, TOO!

IT LOOKS LIKE WE'RE A WHOLE FAMILY AGAIN.

SUCH AS IT IS, YES.

...AND THE TELEVISION'S GONE, TOO.

DO YOU HAPPEN TO HAVE THE SERIAL NUMBER?

I'LL BET THE BURGLARS GOT SCARED OFF WHEN THEY SAW THERE WAS A TIGER IN THE HOUSE! HOBBES WAS HERE THE WHOLE TIME!

CALVIN, NOT NOW, OK? I'M BUSY.

NOBODY STICKS AROUND LONG WHEN HE SEES A TIGER, THAT'S FOR SURE! MANDIBLES OF DEATH, THAT'S WHAT HOBBES HAS!

RIGHT. WHY DON'T YOU GO TELL YOUR MOM?

MAYBE HOBBES SHOULD LOOK AT SOME MUG SHOTS. CAN WE GO TO THE STATION AND IDENTIFY SUSPECTS? HUH, CAN WE?

DEAR!

I SURE MEET THE WEIRDOS IN THIS JOB...

I'VE SWEPT UP MOST OF THE GLASS FROM THE WINDOW.

OK, I'LL GET SOMETHING TO COVER UP THE HOLE.

DO YOU THINK IT'S SAFE TO STAY HERE TONIGHT? SUPPOSE THE BURGLARS COME BACK!

THE POLICE SAID THEY'D DRIVE BY, AND WE'LL LEAVE LOTS OF LIGHTS ON.

UGH, IT'S SO CREEPY KNOWING THESE GOONS HAVE BEEN IN OUR HOUSE. I DON'T FEEL SAFE AT ALL.

I KNOW. AND THIS MUST *REALLY* BE SCARY FOR A LITTLE KID LIKE CALVIN.

GOSH, I CAN'T WAIT TO TELL EVERYONE AT SCHOOL HOW OUR HOUSE GOT ROBBED!

BE SURE TO SAY WHO SCARED THE BURGLARS AWAY AFTER THEY TOOK THE TV AND JEWELRY.

Panel 1: IS CALVIN ASLEEP? — YES, HE'S SNUGGLED UP WITH HOBBES.

Panel 2: BOY, I DON'T KNOW HOW *I'M* EVER GOING TO SLEEP. — ME NEITHER. I CAN'T GET OVER WHAT'S HAPPENED.

Panel 3: THE IDEA OF SOME CRAZY STRANGER GOING THROUGH OUR HOUSE... *BRRRR!!* I WISH *I* HAD A BIG STUFFED ANIMAL TO FEEL SAFE WITH.

Panel 4: I GUESS YOU'LL HAVE TO DO. — SO WHAT DO *I* GET TO SNUGGLE? HOW COME *I'M* THE GROWN-UP??

Panel 5: THIS IS GOING TO BE A LONG NIGHT.

Panel 6: MY HEART JUMPS AT THE SLIGHTEST SOUND. IT'S ALMOST 2, AND I'M WIDE AWAKE.

Panel 7: WHEN SOMEONE BREAKS INTO YOUR HOME, IT SHATTERS YOUR LAST ILLUSION OF SECURITY. IF YOU'RE NOT SAFE IN YOUR OWN HOME, YOU'RE NOT SAFE ANYWHERE.

Panel 8: A MAN'S HOME IS HIS CASTLE, BUT IT SHOULDN'T HAVE TO BE A FORTRESS.

Panel 9: ARE YOU STILL AWAKE TOO? — MM-HMM. I WAS THINKING.

Panel 10: IT'S FUNNY... WHEN I WAS A KID, I THOUGHT GROWN-UPS NEVER WORRIED ABOUT ANYTHING. I TRUSTED MY PARENTS TO TAKE CARE OF EVERYTHING, AND IT NEVER OCCURRED TO ME THAT THEY MIGHT NOT KNOW HOW.

Panel 11: I FIGURED THAT ONCE YOU GREW UP, YOU AUTOMATICALLY KNEW WHAT TO DO IN ANY GIVEN SCENARIO.

Panel 12: I DON'T THINK I'D HAVE BEEN IN SUCH A HURRY TO REACH ADULTHOOD IF I'D KNOWN THE WHOLE THING WAS GOING TO BE AD-LIBBED.

WELL, AT LEAST WE WEREN'T HOME WHEN OUR HOUSE WAS BROKEN INTO. NO ONE WAS HURT. WE'RE ALL TOGETHER AND OK.

WE LOST A FEW OF OUR NICE THINGS, BUT THINGS DON'T MATTER MUCH REALLY.

IT'S HARD TO BELIEVE HOW OFTEN WE FORGET THAT.

CAN I BE EXCUSED NOW?

YOU DIDN'T FINISH YOUR DINNER.

WELL, I DIDN'T LIKE IT VERY MUCH, AND THERE'S THIS TV SHOW I WANT TO WATCH, SO...

OUR TV WAS STOLEN, REMEMBER?

GOSH, I GUESS I'LL EAT MY ASPARAGUS, DO MY HOMEWORK, AND GO STRAIGHT TO BED, THEN.

AND WE'RE SO PROUD OF HOW YOU HANDLE ADVERSITY.

THIS IS WHERE OUR TELEVISION USED TO BE.

BUT WE DON'T HAVE A TV ANYMORE. NOW WE HAVE A BLANK WALL TO WATCH.

SO HERE I AM, NOT BEING ENTERTAINED.

A POINTLESS EXISTENCE, HUH?

I MEAN, THE WALL IS EVEN PLAIN OLD *WHITE*!

CALVIN and HOBBES

by WATTERSON

> I CAN'T SLEEP.

> I THINK NIGHTTIME IS DARK SO YOU CAN IMAGINE YOUR FEARS WITH LESS DISTRACTION.

> AT NIGHTTIME, THE WORLD ALWAYS SEEMS SO BIG AND SCARY, AND I ALWAYS SEEM SO SMALL.

> I WISH I COULD FALL ASLEEP, SO IT WOULD BE MORNING.

> SIGHHHHH...

> LOOK AT HOBBES. *HE'S* ASLEEP.

> HEH HEH... HE SURE LOOKS FUNNY WHEN HE SLEEPS. TIGERS CLOSE THEIR EYES SO TIGHT. I WONDER WHAT HE'S DREAMING ABOUT.

> GOOD OL' HOBBES. WHAT A FRIEND.

> THINGS ARE NEVER QUITE AS SCARY WHEN YOU'VE GOT A BEST FRIEND.

HI, CALVIN! WHAT ARE YOU DOING, MAKING PAPER HATS? CAN I MAKE ONE, TOO?

DON'T BE RIDICULOUS. THIS IS THE OFFICIAL CHAPEAU OF OUR TOP-SECRET CLUB, G.R.O.S.S. — *GET RID OF SLIMY GIRLS!*

"SLIMY GIRLS"?!

I KNOW THAT'S REDUNDANT, BUT OTHERWISE IT DOESN'T SPELL ANYTHING. NOW GO AWAY.

GIRLS AREN'T SLIMY!

DON'T GET GUNK ON ME. I TOOK A BATH LAST SATURDAY AND I'M ALL CLEAN.

I CAN'T BELIEVE YOU STARTED A SECRET CLUB JUST TO EXCLUDE GIRLS! THERE'S NOTHING WRONG WITH GIRLS!

SEE, HOBBES? GIRLS ARE SO EMOTIONAL.

YOU'RE THE MEANEST, MOST ROTTEN LITTLE KID I KNOW! WELL, FINE! PLAY WITH YOUR STUFFED TIGER! SEE WHAT I CARE! I DON'T WANT TO PLAY WITH A STINKER LIKE YOU ANYWAY!!

WOW, WHAT A GREAT CLUB!

OK, WE'VE GOT A SIGN FOR OUR SECRET CLUB, SO NOW WE NEED TO FIND A SECRET MEETING PLACE.

I KNOW! WE CAN SET UP A CARD TABLE IN THE GARAGE! THAT WOULD BE PERFECT FOR DRAWING UP MAPS AND STUFF!

HMM, THERE'S NOT MUCH ROOM WITH THE CAR HERE. LET'S PUSH IT INTO THE DRIVE.

SHOULDN'T YOU ASK YOUR MOM TO MOVE IT INSTEAD?

NAHH. SHE WON'T CARE IF WE PUSH IT OUT. C'MON.

IN THE PAST, YOU'VE BEEN A REMARKABLY POOR JUDGE OF WHAT YOUR MOM CARES ABOUT.

WHAT'S GOING ON, I WONDER. WHY ARE ALL THOSE CARS SLOWING DOWN AS THEY GO BY?

GOSH, DID SOMEONE HAVE AN ACCIDENT? IT LOOKS LIKE THERE'S A CAR IN THE DITCH! ...BUT I DON'T SEE ANYONE BY IT.

AND HOW ON EARTH DID THEY GO IN STRAIGHT BACKWARD? TO DO THAT, THE CAR WOULD'VE HAD TO COME...

...RIGHT...OUT...OUR... DRIVEWAY!

WELL, MOM'S SURE TO HAVE FOUND THE CAR BY NOW AND GUESSED WHAT WE DID.

NOW I KNOW WHAT THEY MEAN WHEN THEY SAY YOU CAN'T GO HOME AGAIN.

WHAT'S THAT SOUND?

I DON'T HEAR ANYTHING.

THERE! SOMETHING IS CRASHING THROUGH THE BRUSH!

IT SOUNDS BIG! MAYBE IT'S A BEAR!

THERE ARE *BEARS* OUT HERE *??*

CLIMB THE TREE! CLIMB THE TREE!

IF YOU ASK *ME*, TIGERS ARE THE ONLY FEROCIOUS ANIMALS THE WORLD REALLY NEEDS.

"BOY, 6, KILLED BY BEAR! PARENTS SAVED THE TROUBLE."

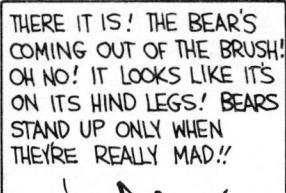

DO YOU THINK WE'RE SAFE? SHOULD WE CLIMB HIGHER?

IT'S HARD TO SAY WITH BEARS.

THERE IT IS! THE BEAR'S COMING OUT OF THE BRUSH! OH NO! IT LOOKS LIKE IT'S ON ITS HIND LEGS! BEARS STAND UP ONLY WHEN THEY'RE REALLY MAD!!

WAIT, THAT'S NOT A BEAR. THAT'S YOUR MOM!

AAUGHH! EVEN WORSE! CLIMB HIGHER! CLIMB HIGHER!

THERE YOU ARE. COME DOWN SO I CAN TALK TO YOU.

NO. YOU'LL KILL US. WE'RE RUNNING AWAY.

I'M NOT GOING TO KILL YOU. I JUST WANT TO FIND OUT WHAT HAPPENED. ARE YOU OK? WAS ANYONE HURT?

NO ONE WAS HURT. WE WERE PUSHING THE CAR INTO THE DRIVE AND IT KEPT ROLLING.

THE CAR DIDN'T HIT ANYTHING?

IT JUST WENT ACROSS THE ROAD AND INTO THE DITCH. THAT'S WHEN WE TOOK OFF.

WELL, THE TOW TRUCK PULLED IT OUT, AND THERE'S NO DAMAGE, SO YOU CAN COME HOME NOW.

FIRST LET'S HEAR YOU SAY YOU LOVE ME.

BOY, HOBBES, ISN'T IT FUNNY HOW THINGS SOMETIMES WORK OUT? MOM AND DAD SAW RIGHT AWAY THAT WHAT HAPPENED TO THE CAR WAS AN ACCIDENT.

THEY WERE SO RELIEVED NO ONE GOT HURT THAT ALL WE GOT WAS A LECTURE ON SAFETY AND ASKING PERMISSION. THEY DIDN'T EVEN RAISE THEIR VOICES.

PARENTS ARE SURE INSCRUTABLE, HUH? SEND THEIR CAR OVER A DITCH AND YOU DON'T EVEN GET YELLED AT.

... BUT TRY KEEPING LIVE WORMS IN YOUR DAD'S...

LET'S NOT TALK ABOUT THAT, OK?!

Calvin and Hobbes

by WATTERSON

TRUE FRIENDS ARE HARD TO COME BY.

I NEED MORE MONEY.

I WISH PEOPLE WERE MORE LIKE ANIMALS.

ANIMALS DON'T TRY TO CHANGE YOU OR MAKE YOU FIT IN. THEY JUST ENJOY THE PLEASURE OF YOUR COMPANY.

ANIMALS AREN'T CONDITIONAL ABOUT FRIENDSHIPS. ANIMALS LIKE YOU JUST THE WAY YOU ARE.

THEY LISTEN TO YOUR PROBLEMS, THEY COMFORT YOU WHEN YOU'RE SAD, AND ALL THEY ASK IN RETURN IS A LITTLE KINDNESS.

WHOONK! *SOB* IT'S SO...SO *TRUE!* HOOOOT! THBPBTPTH!

... AND SPEAKING OF "A LITTLE KINDNESS," I'D HAVE A TUNA FISH SANDWICH ANY TIME SOON THAT YOU HAPPEN TO MAKE ONE...

OF COURSE, *SOME* ANIMALS GET ON YOUR NERVES ONCE IN A WHILE.

Calvin and Hobbes

by WATTERSON

MILD-MANNERED CALVIN IS STUCK INSIDE DOING MATH PROBLEMS ON A BEAUTIFUL SUNDAY.

NO ONE IS WATCHING! HE DASHES INTO HIS CLOSET! *THIS* IS A JOB FOR...

STUPENDOUS MAN! DEFENDER OF FREEDOM! ADVOCATE OF LIBERTY!

A BRIGHT CRIMSON STREAK BLASTS UP THROUGH THE ATMOSPHERE, AND THEN TURNS BACK TOWARD EARTH!

GAINING STUPENDOUS MOMENTUM, *STUPENDOUS MAN* STRIKES THE GROUND AT AN ACUTE ANGLE WITH STUPENDOUS FORCE!

THE EARTH SLOWLY STOPS ROTATING... AND BEGINS TO TURN IN THE OPPOSITE DIRECTION!

PUSHING WITH ALL HIS MIGHT, *STUPENDOUS MAN* TURNS THE PLANET ALL THE WAY AROUND BACKWARD! THE SUN SETS IN THE EAST AND RISES IN THE WEST! SOON IT'S 10 A.M. THE PREVIOUS DAY!

WHAT ARE YOU DOING OUTSIDE? DID YOU FINISH YOUR HOMEWORK ALREADY?

IT'S SATURDAY! I DON'T NEED TO DO IT UNTIL TOMORROW... *THANKS TO STUPENDOUS MAN!*

HERE'S THE LATEST POLL OF HOUSEHOLD 6-YEAR-OLDS, DAD.

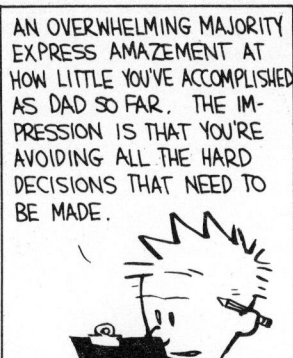

AN OVERWHELMING MAJORITY EXPRESS AMAZEMENT AT HOW LITTLE YOU'VE ACCOMPLISHED AS DAD SO FAR. THE IMPRESSION IS THAT YOU'RE AVOIDING ALL THE HARD DECISIONS THAT NEED TO BE MADE.

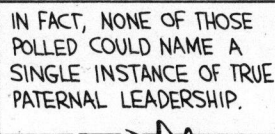

IN FACT, NONE OF THOSE POLLED COULD NAME A SINGLE INSTANCE OF TRUE PATERNAL LEADERSHIP.

HOW ABOUT IF I LEAD YOU UPSTAIRS TO YOUR BED?

HA HA. IF WE CAN BE SERIOUS FOR A MOMENT, I HAVE SOME INNOVATIVE IDEAS ABOUT MY ALLOWANCE.

LOOK AT ALL THESE ANTS.

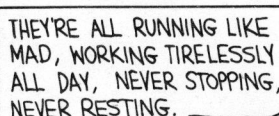

THEY'RE ALL RUNNING LIKE MAD, WORKING TIRELESSLY ALL DAY, NEVER STOPPING, NEVER RESTING.

AND FOR WHAT? TO BUILD A TINY LITTLE HILL OF SAND THAT COULD BE WIPED OUT AT ANY MOMENT! ALL THEIR WORK COULD BE FOR NOTHING, AND YET THEY KEEP ON BUILDING. THEY NEVER GIVE UP!

I SUPPOSE THERE'S A LESSON IN THAT.

YEAH ... ANTS ARE MORONS. LET'S SEE WHAT'S ON TV.

BOY, WHAT A GROUCH.

84

WHERE ARE *YOU* GOING?

OUT.

DID YOU PICK UP YOUR ROOM LIKE I ASKED YOU TO?

NO.

SO WHEN YOU SAY YOU'RE GOING "OUT," YOU REALLY MEAN YOU'RE GOING BACK UPSTAIRS TO CLEAN YOUR ROOM, RIGHT?

ENGLISH MUST NOT BE HER FIRST LANGUAGE.

WHAT ARE YOU DOING DOWN HERE AGAIN? DIDN'T I JUST SEND YOU TO CLEAN YOUR ROOM?!

TWISTED FIEND! NO FOUR WALLS CAN HOLD *STUPENDOUS MAN!* YOU'VE BEEN FOILED AGAIN, EVIL MOM-LADY! HA HA HA!

OH YEAH?

GREAT ZOK! SHE'S FIXED HER MIND-SCRAMBLING EYEBALL RAY ON ME! I'M SUDDENLY FILLED WITH THE DESIRE TO GO BACK UPSTAIRS AND DO HER NEFARIOUS BIDDING!

GLAD TO HEAR IT.

"CLEAN UP YOUR ROOM! CLEAN UP YOUR ROOM!" THAT'S ALL I EVER HEAR!

IT'S *MY* ROOM, RIGHT?!? IF *I* DON'T MIND THE MESS, WHAT BUSINESS IS IT OF ANYONE ELSE?! THIS IS TYRANNY! I *HATE* CLEANING MY ROOM!

IT'S GOING TO TAKE ME ALL *DAY* TO DO THIS! OOH, THIS MAKES ME MAD! A WHOLE DAY SHOT! WASTED! DOWN THE DRAIN! GONE!

AARGH!

ARE YOU KIDDING? HOW COULD THIS POSSIBLY TAKE ALL DAY?

HECK, IT'LL BE ANOTHER HOUR BEFORE I'M EVEN THROUGH GRIPING.

CLEANING MY ROOM WILL GO A LOT FASTER IF WE *BOTH* WORK, RIGHT?

SO I'LL SIT HERE AND DO ALL THE TEDIOUS, AGONIZING PLANNING AND ORGANIZING... ...YOU KNOW, MAKING THE TOUGH CALLS AND THE HARD DECISIONS. YOU WON'T HAVE TO DO ANY OF THAT.

ALL *YOU* DO THEN IS PICK UP WHAT I TELL YOU TO, OK?

HEY! DID I *SAY* TO PICK UP *ME?!* NO, AS A MATTER OF FACT, I DIDN'T! GET AWAY FROM THAT TRASH CAN! *I'M* THE ORGANIZER! *HEY!*

I CLEANED MY STUPID ROOM! CAN I GO OUTSIDE NOW?!

THAT DIDN'T TAKE YOU VERY LONG. LET'S SEE WHAT KIND OF JOB YOU DID.

I DID A *GREAT* JOB! SEE? CAN I GO NOW?

YOUR ROOM LOOKS GOOD. NOW DID YOU STRAIGHTEN UP YOUR CLOSET LIKE I ASKED YOU TO?

AAUGH! DON'T OPEN THAA...

BACK TO WORK, KIDDO.

YOU MADE *THIS* MESS! *YOU* CLEAN IT UP!

WHACK

OUR FAVORITE GAMES ARE THE ONES WE DON'T UNDERSTAND!

YOU MISSED A WICKET! NO GOAL! NO GOAL!

 HELP! A BEE! A BEE! RUN FOR YOUR LIFE!

HOBBES! DID YOU SEE IT?? IT WAS THE BIGGEST BEE IN THE WORLD! IT WAS THE SIZE OF A KAISER ROLL! IT MUST'VE WEIGHED 70 POUNDS!

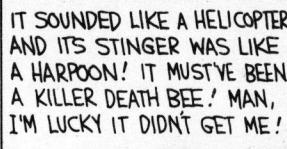
IT SOUNDED LIKE A HELICOPTER AND ITS STINGER WAS LIKE A HARPOON! IT MUST'VE BEEN A KILLER DEATH BEE! MAN, I'M LUCKY IT DIDN'T GET ME!

LIFE IN THE GREAT SUBURBAN OUTBACK IS CERTAINLY FRAUGHT WITH PERIL.

IF YOU'D SEEN IT, YOU'D HAVE BEEN SCARED, TOO.

I CAN'T IMAGINE MASTERING THE SKILLS INVOLVED HERE WITHOUT A CLEARER UNDERSTANDING OF WHO'S GOING TO BE IMPRESSED.

I SAW THE MAN IN THE MOON TONIGHT.

MM.

I DIDN'T KNOW THE MOON MADE FACES.

THAT'S "PHASES."

CALVIN and HOBBES

by WATTERSON

AHHHH...

UH-OH. SOMETHING IS SERIOUSLY WRONG HERE.

THE LAWS OF PERSPECTIVE HAVE BEEN REPEALED!

OBJECTS NO LONGER DIMINISH IN SIZE WITH DISTANCE!

LINES DO NOT CONVERGE TOWARD ANY POINT ON THE HORIZON!

ALL SPATIAL RELATIONSHIPS ARE LOST! ITS IMPOSSIBLE TO JUDGE WHERE ANYTHING IS! OH NO!

CALVIN, QUIT RUNNING AROUND AND CRASHING INTO THINGS, OR I'LL SELL YOU TO THE MONKEY HOUSE!

...AND NOW *SHE'S* LOST PERSPECTIVE.

CALVIN and HOBBES
by WATTERSON

z

AAUGH! GRRRRRR

WHAM!

YOU CAN TAKE THE TIGER OUT OF THE JUNGLE, BUT YOU CAN'T TAKE THE JUNGLE OUT OF THE TIGER!

THE QUESTION *IS*, HOW CAN YOU GET THE TIGER *BACK* IN THE JUNGLE?

IT'S JULY ALREADY! OH NO! OH NO!

WHAT HAPPENED TO JUNE?! SUMMER VACATION IS SLIPPING THROUGH OUR FINGERS LIKE GRAINS OF SAND!

IT'S GOING TOO FAST! WE'VE GOT TO HOARD OUR FREEDOM AND HAVE MORE FUN! TIME RUSHES ON! HELP! HELP!

I DON'T THINK I WANT TO BE HERE AT THE END OF AUGUST.

AAUGH! IT'S A HALF-HOUR LATER THAN IT WAS HALF AN HOUR AGO! RUN! RUN!

MOM TOOK ME TO THE LIBRARY TODAY, DAD.

THAT'S NICE. DID YOU GET OUT A BOOK?

YEP. IT'S GREAT! I HAD NO IDEA BOOKS COULD BE SO MUCH FUN.

AND YOU'LL LEARN THINGS, TOO.

I'LL SAY! MY BOOK SAYS THAT THIS ONE WASP LAYS ITS EGG ON A SPIDER, SO WHEN THE EGG HATCHES, THE LARVA EATS THE SPIDER, SAVING THE VITAL ORGANS FOR LAST, SO THE SPIDER STAYS ALIVE WHILE IT'S BEING DEVOURED!

GROSS, HUH?

ISN'T THERE A STREET CORNER WHERE HE COULD HANG OUT INSTEAD?

AND COLOR PICTURES, TOO! WANT TO SEE 'EM?

I'M DESTINED FOR GREATNESS, I JUST KNOW IT. "CALVIN THE GREAT," THEY'LL CALL ME.

AND THINK HOW LUCKY *YOU'LL* BE! YOU'LL GET TO TELL EVERYONE HOW YOU KNEW ME AS A KID! WHAT A PRIVILEGE!

IN FACT, ALL THE PAPERS AND MAGAZINES WILL PROBABLY WANT TO INTERVIEW YOU TO FIND OUT WHAT I'M REALLY LIKE.

AND BOY, WILL YOU HAVE TO COUGH UP TO KEEP ME QUIET.

AND WHAT'S *THAT* SUPPOSED TO MEAN?!

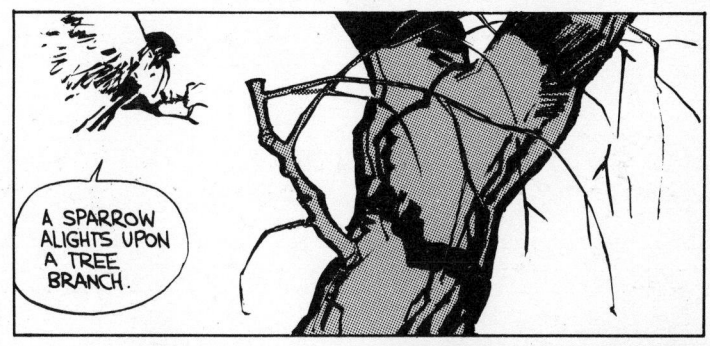

DAD, HOW DOES A LIGHT BULB WORK?

MAGIC.

DIDN'T YOU SAY THAT'S HOW THE VACUUM CLEANER WORKS?

RIGHT. THEY'RE BOTH MAGIC.

YOU JUST DON'T *KNOW* HOW THEY WORK, I'LL BET.

FINE. DON'T BELIEVE YOUR OWN FATHER, WHO'S BEEN AROUND A LOT LONGER THAN YOU.

LOOK MOM, MAGIC!

THAT'S NOT MAGIC!

WHEN YOU WISH UPON A STAR YOUR DREAMS COME TRUE.

I WISH I HAD A COOL MILLION DOLLARS RIGHT NOW!

IF JIMINY CRICKET WAS HERE, I'D SKOOSH HIM.

WHAP

I DID IT! I CAUGHT IT!

I'M OUT.

WUM WUM WUM

HOW'S IT GOING?

FINE. CLOSE THE LID. EVERYTHING STOPS WHEN YOU OPEN IT.

I WISH *MY* BATHTUB HAD AN AGITATOR.

CALVIN, WILL YOU GATHER THE TRASH, PLEASE?

GATHER THE *TRASH*?!? WHAT AM I, YOUR PERSONAL *SLAVE*?! WHY CAN'T *YOU* DO IT?

FINE, I WILL. AND *YOU* CAN START WASHING YOUR *OWN* CLOTHES, AND FIXING YOUR *OWN* MEALS, AND PICKING UP YOUR *OWN* TOYS, AND MAKING YOUR *OWN* BED, AND CLEANING UP YOUR *OWN* MESSES, DAY AFTER DAY AFTER *DAY*!

SOME WOMEN JUST WEREN'T MEANT TO BE MOTHERS.

WHENEVER I COOK AN EGG, I LIKE TO SEE HOW HIGH I CAN CRACK IT ABOVE THE SKILLET.

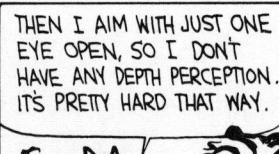

THEN I AIM WITH JUST ONE EYE OPEN, SO I DON'T HAVE ANY DEPTH PERCEPTION. IT'S PRETTY HARD THAT WAY.

SEE, THE SECRET TO HAVING FUN IN LIFE IS TO MAKE LITTLE CHALLENGES FOR YOURSELF.

CRIKK

LIKE THE CHALLENGE OF EXPLAINING THE STOVE AND FLOOR TO YOUR MOM?

RATS. SEE IF THERE'S ANOTHER CARTON IN THE FRIDGE, WILL YA?

CALVIN and HOBBES

by WATTERSON

CLICK

UH OH...

THE SKY IS A DEEP ORANGE! CALVIN'S SKIN IS A PALE GREEN! YELLOW FLOWERS ARE NOW BLUE!

EVERY COLOR IS THE OPPOSITE OF WHAT IT SHOULD BE!

CALVIN HAS BEEN TRANSFERRED TO A COLOR FILM NEGATIVE!

HIS ONLY HOPE IS TO BE PROCESSED BY A 1-HOUR PHOTO FINISHER! DEVELOPER! I NEED DEVELOPER!

DOGGONE IT, CALVIN! THAT'S *ANOTHER* PICTURE RUINED! CAN'T YOU LOOK PLEASANT FOR 1/500TH OF A SECOND?!

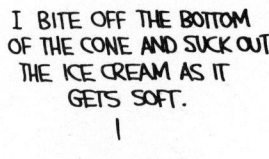

Panel 1: WELL, THERE'S NO DELAYING THE INEVITABLE. LET'S GET IN THE CAR.

Panel 2: WHERE ARE WE GOING?

THE SAME PLACE WE GO *EVERY* SUMMER: CAMPING ON SOME DESOLATE ROCK AT THE END OF THE EARTH.

Panel 3: *AGAIN?*

YEP. THIS IS HOW DAD LIKES TO UNWIND.

Panel 4: WITH EVERYONE COMPLAINING?

RIGHT. HE LIKES TO WATCH US ALL SUFFER.

Panel 5: LOOK, DAD, THERE'S A TOWN COMING UP. SEE THE SIGN?

Panel 6: WHY DON'T WE PULL OFF, FIND A NICE MOTEL AND JUST STAY *THERE* FOR OUR VACATION? WE COULD SWIM IN THE POOL AND HAVE AIR CONDITIONING AND COLOR CABLE TV AND ROOM SERVICE!

Panel 7: NO ONE WOULD HAVE TO KNOW WE DIDN'T CAMP! *I* WOULDN'T TELL ANYONE! WE COULD EVEN GO TO THE STORE, BUY A BIG FISH, TAKE YOUR PICTURE WITH IT, AND SAY YOU CAUGHT IT! CAN'T WE, DAD? CAN'T WE TURN OFF HERE?

Panel 8: YES, LET'S!

NOW DON'T *YOU* START!

Panel 9: TA DA! WE'RE HERE!

GOOD OL' "ITCHY ISLAND," HOME OF THE NUCLEAR MOSQUITOES.

Panel 10: BUG BITES BUILD CHARACTER.

YEAH, AND LAST YEAR YOU SAID DIARRHEA BUILDS CHARACTER.

Panel 11: SO THINK WHAT A FINE YOUNG MAN YOU'RE GROWING UP TO BE.

...IF ALL THIS CHARACTER DOESN'T KILL ME FIRST.

Panel 12: THAT REMINDS ME, OPEN THE DUFFEL BAG AND GET OUT THE SPAM.

IF THE CANOE ISN'T HERE IN THE MORNING, IT MEANS HOBBES AND I STRUCK OUT FOR HOME.

BOY, IT'S GREAT TO BE HERE! THIS IS THE LIFE! I THINK I'LL JUMP IN FOR A SWIM. WANT TO JOIN ME?

NO, THANKS.

AW, C'MON. IT'LL FEEL GREAT.

RIGHT. THAT LAKE COULDN'T HAVE MELTED BEFORE YESTERDAY.

HEY, LET'S GO FOR A SWIM!

SURE, DAD. I'D LOVE TO START THE WEEK WITH A LITTLE HYPOTHERMIA.

I THINK WHAT I LIKE BEST ABOUT VACATIONS IS THE FAMILY TOGETHERNESS.

WAKE UP, CALVIN. IT'S 5:30 AND YOU CAN SEE THE FISH JUMPING.

MMF. GOWAY.

IT'S A BEAUTIFUL MORNING. THE SUN'S BARELY UP AND THERE'S A MIST OVER THE WATER. IT'S PERFECTLY STILL. NOT A SOUL ANYWHERE! DON'T YOU WANT TO SEE THIS?

LEEMEE LONE.

I THOUGHT YOU SAID YOU WANTED TO GO FISHING. YOU'VE GOT TO GET UP EARLY IF YOU WANT TO CATCH ANYTHING. C'MON, THE CANOE'S ALL READY AND I'VE GOT YOUR FISHING ROD.

MOM, MAKE DAD GO AWAY!

ANOTHER THING I LIKE ABOUT VACATIONS IS THE SHARING OF SPECIAL MOMENTS.

WELL, I GUESS THAT'S ENOUGH FISHING FOR NOW. MMM, I CAN'T WAIT TO GET BACK AND HAVE BREAKFAST! I CAN ALMOST SMELL THE COFFEE FROM HERE! WHAT A LIFE!

HEY, WHERE *IS* EVERY...

THERE'S GOING TO BE A SMALL MOUTH BASS FLOPPING IN SOME SLEEPING BAGS IN A MINUTE OR TWO!

YOU KNOW, I REALLY LIKE IT WHEN YOU GO OFF TO WORK IN THE MORNINGS.

IT'S 6:30 ALREADY! ARE YOU PEOPLE GOING TO WASTE THE WHOLE DAY?

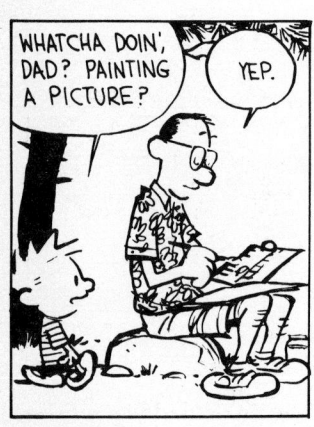

OOH, THESE BUGS ARE AWFUL! I ITCH ALL OVER!

DON'T SCRATCH THE BITES OR YOU'LL JUST MAKE THE ITCHING WORSE.

WHAT AM I SUPPOSED TO DO THEN? IT'S DRIVING ME CRAZY!

THINK ABOUT SOMETHING ELSE.

SOMETHING ELSE?! LIKE WHAT??

LIKE MAYBE STEPPING OUT OF ALL THAT POISON IVY.

I HATE THIS PLACE!

OK, GANG, SMILE!

ACK! DON'T TAKE A PICTURE OF ME! I HAVEN'T WASHED MY HAIR IN THREE DAYS AND I'M COVERED WITH BUG BITES!

BUT DON'T YOU WANT SOMETHING TO REMEMBER OUR TRIP BY?

I DON'T WANT TO REMEMBER THIS TRIP! I'VE BEEN TRYING TO FORGET IT EVER SINCE WE GOT HERE! WHEN ARE WE LEAVING THIS DUMP?

THE NEXT TIME I SEE ONE OF THOSE SMARMY KODAK COMMERCIALS I'M GOING TO PUT AN AX THROUGH THE TV.

THIS VACATION SURE WENT QUICKLY. I CAN'T BELIEVE IT'S TIME TO GO HOME SO SOON.

AFTER BEING OUT HERE, IT WILL SURE BE A CULTURE SHOCK TO GO BACK TO CIVILIZATION, WON'T IT?

MAN, I CAN'T WAIT TO GET IN THE CAR AND CRANK UP THE A/C AND SOME TUNES. SHAKE A LEG, HUH?

SOMEDAY I'M GOING TO GET MY DNA TESTED AND SEE IF HE'S REALLY MY KID.

TAKE MY WORD FOR IT.

CALVIN and HOBBES
by WATTERSON

HEH HEH HEH...

YOU'RE IN TROUBLE *NOW*, HOBBES! HEH HEH HEH!

WHILE YOU HAVE JUST *ONE* WATER BALLOON, I HAVE *THREE!* I'M A WALKING ARSENAL OF HYDRO-WEAPONRY!

HA HA! I CAN SEE THE FEAR IN YOUR EYES! YOU REALIZE THAT I CAN GET YOU THREE TIMES WETTER THAN YOU CAN GET ME!

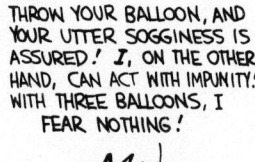

THROW YOUR BALLOON, AND YOUR UTTER SOGGINESS IS ASSURED! *I*, ON THE OTHER HAND, CAN ACT WITH IMPUNITY! WITH THREE BALLOONS, I FEAR NOTHING!

CATCH.

HEY! DON'T! MY ARMS ARE FULL!

OH NO!

SPLOOSH GISSHH SPLASH FWOOSH

WE SUPER-POWERS HAVE IT TOUGH.

MAYBE YOU SHOULD STOCK UP ON BRAINS INSTEAD!

calvin and hobbes

by WATTERSON

AHH... A DAY AT THE LAKE! THIS WILL BE GREAT!

I STILL DON'T SEE WHY WE CAN'T JUST SIT IN THE CAR WITH THE AIR CONDITIONER ON.

I'M GETTING SAND IN MY SUIT! I DON'T WANT TO SIT ON THE BEACH!

THIS WATER'S TOO COLD! I'M FREEZING TO DEATH!

OUT HERE THERE'S TOO MUCH SUN! I'LL GET SUNBURNED!

THIS LOTION MAKES ME GREASY AND MY SHIRT MAKES ME TOO HOT!

I DON'T WANT TO SIT IN THE SHADE! THIS IS BORING!

I HATE WALKING! MY LEGS ARE TIRED AND THE SAND IS TOO HOT AND THE WATER IS TOO COLD AND THERE'S NO SHADE HERE AND I'VE STILL GOT SAND IN MY SUIT!

WHAT? ARE WE GOING ALREADY?

ARR! WE'RE BLOODTHIRSTY PIRATES!

AVAST, YE SCURVY DOGS! HOIST THE JOLLY ROGER AND READY THE PLANK!

HERE.

WHAT'S THIS?

OUR BOOTY!

HEY, MOM, DID YOU KNOW THAT GRAVITY IN OUTER SPACE WORKS AS IF SPACE WAS A SOFT, FLAT SURFACE? IT'S TRUE.

HEAVY MATTER, LIKE PLANETS, SINKS INTO THE SURFACE AND ANYTHING PASSING BY, LIKE LIGHT, WILL "ROLL" TOWARD THE DIP IN SPACE MADE BY THE PLANET. LIGHT IS ACTUALLY DEFLECTED BY GRAVITY! AMAZING, HUH?

AND SPEAKING OF GRAVITY, I DROPPED A PITCHER OF LEMONADE ON THE KITCHEN FLOOR WHEN MY ROLLER SKATES SLIPPED.

HOW CAN KIDS KNOW SO MUCH AND STILL BE SO DUMB?

YOU KNOW, THE WORLD SHOULD'VE BEEN DESIGNED SO EVERYONE DIDN'T HAVE TO EAT EACH OTHER TO SURVIVE. THERE SHOULD JUST BE FEWER PEOPLE AND ANIMALS TO BEGIN WITH.

AND THE WORLD CERTAINLY COULD'VE USED A MORE EVEN DISTRIBUTION OF ITS RESOURCES, THAT'S FOR SURE.

I WONDER WHY NOBODY CONSULTED YOU.

INCREDIBLE, ISN'T IT?

I PERFORMED A SCIENTIFIC EXPERIMENT TODAY.

YOU KNOW HOW MAPS ALWAYS SHOW NORTH AS UP AND SOUTH AS DOWN? I WANTED TO SEE IF THAT WAS TRUE OR NOT.

WHAT DID YOU FIND OUT?

NOT MUCH. YOUR COMPASS DIDN'T SURVIVE THE TRIP SOUTH FROM THE TOP OF THE TREE.

MY COMPASS?!

LET ME KNOW WHEN YOU GET A NEW ONE. MY JUNIOR SCIENTIST BOOK SAYS NOT TO GET DISCOURAGED BY TEMPORARY SETBACKS.

I'VE BEEN THINKING. YOU KNOW HOW BORING DAD IS? MAYBE IT'S A BIG PHONY ACT!

MAYBE AFTER HE PUTS US TO BED, DAD DONS SOME WEIRD COSTUME AND GOES OUT FIGHTING CRIME! MAYBE THIS WHOLE "DAD" STUFF IS JUST A SECRET IDENTITY!

MAYBE THE MAYOR CALLS DAD ON A SECRET HOT LINE WHENEVER THE CITY'S IN TROUBLE! MAYBE DAD'S A MASKED SUPERHERO!

IF THAT'S TRUE HE SHOULD DRIVE A COOLER CAR.

I KNOW. OURS DOESN'T EVEN HAVE A CASSETTE DECK.

THERE'S THE STEGOSAURUS OUT FRONT! THERE'S THE NATURAL HISTORY MUSEUM! HOORAY!

I CAN'T WAIT TO SEE ALL THE DINOSAURS! C'MON, LET'S HURRY!

IT'S CERTAINLY BEEN A WHILE SINCE WE'VE BEEN HERE, HASN'T IT?

AT THE MUSEUM'S REQUEST, YES.

OH, THAT'S RIGHT. CALVIN, NO BITING PEOPLE THIS TIME, REMEMBER?

RROWRR

WHAT KIND OF DINOSAUR DID YOU SAY THIS WAS?

IT'S A STEGO-SAURUS!

HE LOOKS PRETTY FEROCIOUS.

NO, HE WAS A PLANT EATER. THE TAIL SPIKES WERE FOR SELF-DEFENSE.

OH. DID TYRANNOSAURS FIGHT THESE?

OF COURSE NOT, MOM! TYRANNOSAURS CAME MILLIONS OF YEARS LATER!

LOOK, TRY NOT TO EMBARRASS ME WHEN WE GO INSIDE, OK?

WHY ARE WE GOING HERE IF HE ALREADY KNOWS EVERY-THING?

LOOK, HOBBES, HERE'S AN ANCESTOR OF *YOURS!* A SABER-TOOTHED TIGER!

HA HA, I'LL BET *HE* WAS POPULAR! IF ANYONE NEEDED TO OPEN A CAN OF JUICE, THEY'D JUST PUT HIM OVER IT AND HIT HIM ON THE HEAD! HA HA!

HEE HEE, I'LL BET THEY DIED OUT BECAUSE THEY COULDN'T UNDERSTAND EACH OTHER! THEY PWOBABBY DOKKED WIKE DIFF! HA HA HA!

... ALL IN ALL, THOUGH, THEY WERE UNDOUBTEDLY THE PINNACLE OF PREHISTORIC EVOLUTION ..

LOOK, MOM, THE MUSEUM HAS A GIFT SHOP!

CAN I BUY SOMETHING? THEY'VE GOT DINOSAUR BOOKS, DINOSAUR MODELS, DINOSAUR T-SHIRTS, DINOSAUR POSTERS..

I DON'T THINK YOU NEED ANY MORE DINOSAUR STUFF, CALVIN.

BUT MOM, IT'S ALL *EDUCATIONAL!* YOU WANT ME TO *LEARN*, DON'T YOU??

BOY, SHE FELL FOR *THAT* ONE.

I'LL SAY! I WONDER IF WE COULD GET ANY BATMAN JUNK THIS WAY.

Calvin and Hobbes by Watterson

THERE! A FULL PITCHER OF "CALVIN'S CURATIVE ELIXIR"! WE'LL CHARGE PEOPLE A BUCK A GLASS AND GET RICH!

BUT THAT'S JUST DIRTY WATER FROM THE DRAINAGE DITCH! THERE ARE LEAVES IN IT!

"FORTIFIED WITH CHLOROPHYLL," WE'LL SAY.

NOBODY'S GOING TO PAY TO DRINK THAT! ANYONE CAN SEE IT'S FILTHY! IT'S SLUDGE!

HMM... MAYBE YOU'RE RIGHT.

PITCHER OF PLAGUE
CALVIN'S DEBILITATING DISEASE DRINK! $1.00 NOT TO HAVE ANY

I'VE DECIDED NOT TO GO TO SCHOOL THIS FALL.

I DON'T NEED AN EDUCATION. I DON'T NEED TO LEARN THINGS. I DON'T NEED TO DEVELOP SKILLS. IT'S TOO MUCH TROUBLE.

HOW ARE YOU GOING TO MAKE IT IN THE WORLD IF YOU DON'T KNOW ANYTHING AND YOU DON'T HAVE ANY SKILLS?!

I'LL GO ON TALK SHOWS AND HYPE MYSELF.

UGHH, THERE ARE TIMES WHEN I HATE OWNING A HOUSE. ALL THE MAINTENANCE!

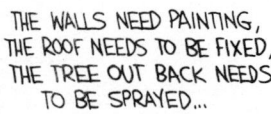

THE WALLS NEED PAINTING, THE ROOF NEEDS TO BE FIXED, THE TREE OUT BACK NEEDS TO BE SPRAYED...

IT SEEMS LIKE THE WHOLE PLACE IS FALLING APART.

... AND WHAT ISN'T FALLING APART IS BEING ACTIVELY DESTROYED!

A 30-TON BRONTOSAURUS

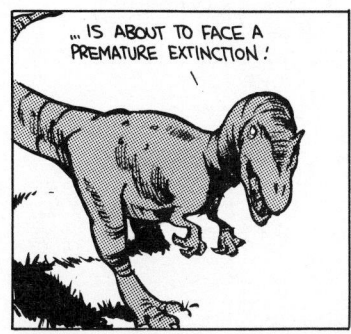

... IS ABOUT TO FACE A PREMATURE EXTINCTION!

THE ALLOSAURUS, FEARSOME PREDATOR OF THE JURASSIC, STALKS HIS PREY!

THE HERD OF BRONTOSAURS IS UNAWARE OF HIS PRESENCE!

SPOTTING A STRAGGLER, THE ALLOSAURUS LUNGES!

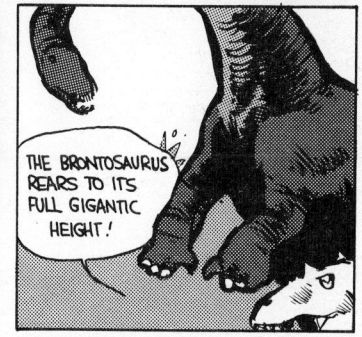

THE BRONTOSAURUS REARS TO ITS FULL GIGANTIC HEIGHT!

WHAT INDUCES AN ALLOSAURUS TO ATTACK A MONSTER MORE THAN TWICE HIS OWN SIZE??

I'M HUNGRY!

THE HAMBURGERS ARE COOKING! NOW GET OFF ME!

CALVIN THE HUMMINGBIRD ZIPS BY WITH A LOUD WHIR!

ALTHOUGH SMALL, HE PUTS OUT TREMENDOUS ENERGY. TO HOVER, HIS WINGS BEAT HUNDREDS OF TIMES EACH SECOND!

WHAT FUELS THIS INCREDIBLE METABOLISM? CONCENTRATED SUGAR WATER! HE DRINKS HALF HIS WEIGHT A DAY.'

...PREFERABLY LOADED WITH CAFFEINE.

ARE YOU DRINKING MORE SODA POP?!

SLURRPP

"ONCE UPON A TIME THERE WAS..."

HOLD IT.

WHAT'S THE MATTER?

HAS THIS BOOK BEEN A BEST SELLER? HAS THE AUTHOR WON A PULITZER? DID THE NEW YORK TIMES LIKE IT?

I ONLY WANT STORIES THAT COME HIGHLY RECOMMENDED. ARE THERE ANY LAUDATORY QUOTES ON THE DUST JACKET?

AHEM... "ONCE UPON A TIME THERE WAS A NOISY KID WHO STARTED GOING TO BED WITHOUT A STORY."

HAS THIS BOOK BEEN MADE INTO A MOVIE? COULD WE BE WATCHING THIS ON VIDEO?

WHAT ARE YOU DOING?

I'M PRACTICING MY SNEERS.

THERE'S NOTHING LIKE A GOOD SNEER TO DRY UP CONVERSATION. HOW'S MINE LOOK?

AWFUL!

THANKS. WITH THIS SNEER, I HOPE TO BE AN UNBEARABLE BURDEN AT ANY SOCIAL OCCASION.

THAT WILL GIVE YOU A REAL HEAD START ON BEING A TEEN-AGER.

I KNOW! IT'S LIKE GETTING SEVEN EXTRA YEARS!

WHAP!

TOO LATE! I MADE ANOTHER HOME RUN.

(PANT PANT) I'M QUITTING IF WE DON'T STOP USING THIS TENNIS BALL.

AAAGH!!

YOU SHOULD BE MORE ALERT! YOU WOULDN'T LAST TWO SECONDS IN THE JUNGLE.

THAT'S WHY I LIVE *HERE*, YOU DOLT!

WHAT ARE YOU DOING DOWN THERE, CALVIN?

SHH, MOM! GO AWAY! SUSIE'S COMING DOWN THE WALK AND I'M GOING TO THROW SOME CRAB APPLES AT HER.

OH, NO, YOU'RE NOT! PUT THOSE DOWN!

AWWW, MOM!

DON'T THROW CRAB APPLES AT *ANY*ONE. THEY'RE HARD AND YOU COULD REALLY HURT SOMEONE.

OK, OK.

WHAT ARE YOU DOING DOWN THERE, CALVIN?

SHH, SUSIE! GO AWAY! I'M GOING TO THROW THIS SQUISHY OLD TOMATO AT MY MOM.

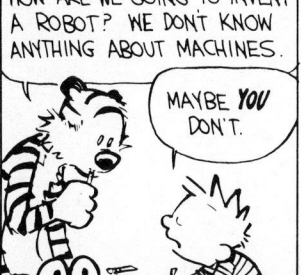

OK, THE FIRST THING OUR ROBOT NEEDS IS A HEAD.

SHOULD WE USE A COFFEE CAN?

NO, THAT'S TOO SMALL. THE HEAD HAS TO HOLD THIS TAPE RECORDER. SEE, I'VE MADE RECORDINGS FOR THE ROBOT'S VOICE!

REALLY?

SURE! THIS WAY, OUR ROBOT NOT ONLY COMMUNICATES, BUT WE CAN ALSO "PROGRAM" HIM TO HAVE THE PROPER PERSONALITY!

PERSONALITY?

RIGHT. ROBOTS SHOULD BE *RESPECTFUL*.

CLICK HOW MAY I EASE YOUR LIFE, OH GRAND EXALTED MASTER?

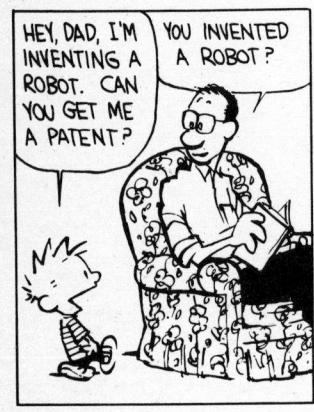

HEY, DAD, I'M INVENTING A ROBOT. CAN YOU GET ME A PATENT?

YOU INVENTED A ROBOT?

WELL, HERE IT IS SO FAR. HOBBES AND I HAVE BEEN WORKING ON IT ALL AFTERNOON. IT'S NOT QUITE PERFECTED YET, BUT YOU GET THE IDEA.

HMM...WHAT DOES IT DO?

THAT'S THE PROBLEM. WE HAVEN'T FIGURED OUT HOW TO MAKE IT DO WHAT WE WANT.

DON'T GET DISCOURAGED. YOUR MOM AND I GOT THE SAME RESULTS AFTER WORKING ON *YOU* FOR SIX *YEARS*.

HAR HAR. MY ATTORNEY IS A COMEDIAN.

WELL, HOBBES, WE MIGHT AS WELL GIVE UP. I CAN'T FIGURE OUT HOW TO MAKE A ROBOT. THIS ONE DOESN'T DO ANYTHING.

IT'S PAST YOUR BEDTIME, CALVIN. YOU'LL HAVE TO LEAVE YOUR TOYS FOR TOMORROW.

OK, MOM. OUR ROBOT WASN'T WORKING OUT ANYWAY.

GOSH, AND WE SPENT ALL DAY ON IT, TOO. I THOUGHT FOR SURE OUR ROBOT WOULD SAVE US FROM MAKING THE BED.

AND IN A WAY, HE *DID*!

HEY, YEAH! WE'RE GENIUSES!

Panel 1: YOUR MOM SURE WAS CHEERFUL THIS MORNING. HMPH.

Panel 2: I'VE NEVER SEEN HER HUMMING AND SASHAYING AROUND THE KITCHEN LIKE THAT. HMPH.

Panel 3: HOW LONG HAVE WE BEEN WAITING FOR THE BUS NOW?

Panel 4: ABOUT TWO AND A HALF HOURS. *I* THINK MOM PUT ME OUT HERE THIS EARLY ON *PURPOSE.*

Panel 5: HI, CALVIN! AREN'T YOU EXCITED ABOUT GOING TO SCHOOL? LOOK AT ALL THESE GREAT SCHOOL SUPPLIES I GOT! I LOVE HAVING NEW NOTEBOOKS AND STUFF!

Panel 6: ALL *I'VE* GOT TO SAY IS THEY'RE NOT MAKING *ME* LEARN ANY FOREIGN LANGUAGES! IF ENGLISH IS GOOD ENOUGH FOR *ME,* THEN BY GOLLY, IT'S GOOD ENOUGH FOR THE *REST* OF THE WORLD!

Panel 7: EVERYONE SHOULD SPEAK ENGLISH OR JUST SHUT UP, THAT'S WHAT *I* SAY!

Panel 8: YOU SHOULD MAYBE CHECK THE CHEMICAL CONTENT OF YOUR BREAKFAST CEREAL. THEY CAN MAKE ME GO UNTIL GRADE EIGHT, AND THEN, *FFFT,* I'M OUTTA HERE!

Panel 9: CALVIN, WOULD YOU LEAD THE CLASS IN THE PLEDGE OF ALLEGIANCE? NO!!

Panel 10: WHAT DID THE SUPREME COURT DECIDE ABOUT THAT? IS THIS A PRAYER? DON'T YOU HAVE TO READ ME MY RIGHTS? I DON'T KEEP UP WITH THIS STUFF! I'M JUST A KID!

Panel 11: I'M ONLY HERE BECAUSE MY PARENTS MAKE ME GO! I DON'T WANT TO BE A TEST CASE! I DON'T EVEN KNOW WHAT COURT DISTRICT I'M IN! CALL ON SOMEONE ELSE!

Panel 12: CALVIN? * SIGHHHH * I CAN'T BELIEVE IT'S NOT EVEN 8:15 YET.

THE FEARLESS SPACEMAN SPIFF IS BEING PURSUED ACROSS THE GALAXY BY DREADED SCUM BEINGS!

THEY'RE GAINING! SPIFF'S ONLY CHANCE TO LOSE THEM IS TO RELEASE A GIANT SMOKE CLOUD BEHIND HIS SPACECRAFT! OUR HERO THROWS THE LEVER!

HEH HEH... JUST UH, CLAPPING THE ERASERS, HEH HEH... (COUGH)

YOU AGAIN?

SIGHHHH I CAN'T BELIEVE IT'S NOT EVEN 8:30 YET.

WHAT A DAY.

I'M HO-O-AAAH!

KAPOINWW!!

THINGS GET SO DARN QUIET WHEN YOU'RE NOT AROUND.

THERE'S GOING TO BE SOME RUCKUS *NOW*, BUDDY-BOY!

IS IT? IT *IS*! IT'S **SATURDAY**! OH BOY!

NO SCHOOL! NO HOMEWORK! JUST CARTOONS AND FUN THE WHOLE DAY LONG!

HOORAY!

TURN ON THE TV! GET OUT THE CEREAL!

IT'S SAAAAT URDAY!

BONK

YOU'RE GETTING UP?? IT'S BARELY LIGHT OUT!

I'M GOING TO THE OFFICE AND GET SOME SLEEP.

CALViN and HOBBES
by WATTERSON

CALVIN?
CALVIN?
CALVIN!

HMM... THE ENGINE'S MAKING FUNNY NOISES..

SPACEMAN SPIFF IS GOING DOWN OVER PLANET GORK!

ZOUNDS! THE PLANET IS INHABITED! AN ALIEN METROPOLIS OPENS UP BEFORE OUR HERO'S EYES!

SPIFF'S STABILIZERS REFUSE TO RESPOND! OUR HERO IS GOING TO CRASH!

THIS SPELLS DISASTER!

CALVIN!

"UH... D... I... S... A... S... T... E... R.

VERY GOOD. I'M GLAD YOU WERE PAYING ATTENTION.

YES! ONCE AGAIN THE INCREDIBLE SPACEMAN SPIFF BEATS ALL ODDS TO SAVE THE DAY!

YOU MAY SIT DOWN, CALVIN.

 UH OH, CALVIN THE REPTILE IS IN TROUBLE!

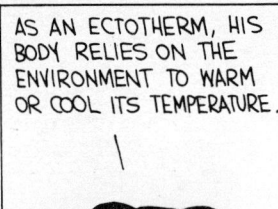 AS AN ECTOTHERM, HIS BODY RELIES ON THE ENVIRONMENT TO WARM OR COOL ITS TEMPERATURE.

 NOW THAT IT'S COLDER OUTSIDE, CALVIN'S BODY TEMPERATURE FALLS AND HE BECOMES SLUGGISH! HE'LL GO INTO TORPOR IF HE CAN'T FIND A WARM PLACE TO LIE!

 LEAVE THE THERMOSTAT ALONE, AND PUT ON A SWEATER IF YOU'RE COLD.

I...I DON'T HAVE THE EN..ENERGY!

I HEARD THAT BIG CATS DON'T PURR.

THAT'S TRUE. WE'RE TOO FIERCE AND FEROCIOUS. WE DON'T EVER PURR.

WELL WHAT DO YOU CALL THE NOISE YOU MAKE WHEN YOU GET YOUR TUMMY RUBBED?!

GROWLING FRIENDLY-LIKE.

 CALVIN, YOUR MOM AND I LOOKED OVER YOUR REPORT CARD, AND WE THINK YOU COULD BE DOING BETTER.

BUT I DON'T LIKE SCHOOL.

 WHY NOT? YOU LIKE TO READ AND YOU LIKE TO LEARN. I KNOW YOU DO.

 I MEAN, YOU'VE READ EVERY DINOSAUR BOOK EVER WRITTEN, AND YOU'VE LEARNED A LOT, RIGHT? READING AND LEARNING ARE FUN.

YEAH..

 SO WHY DON'T YOU LIKE SCHOOL?

WE DON'T READ ABOUT DINOSAURS.

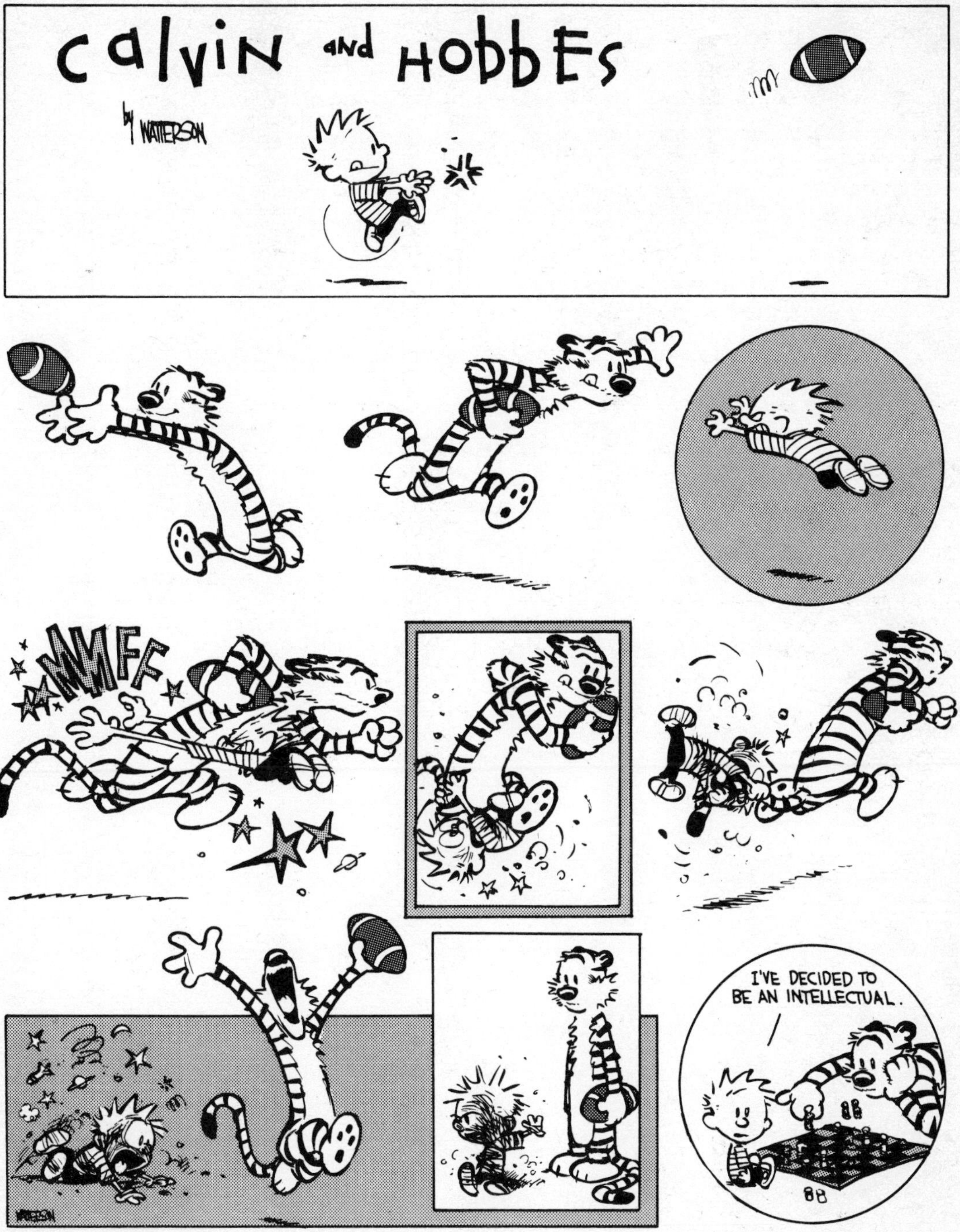

Calvin and Hobbes

by WATTERSON

I'VE DECIDED TO BE AN INTELLECTUAL.

The End